1

Table of Contents

INTRODUCTION

The SIFT exam, or "Selection Instrument for Flight Training" is utilized by the Army to determine if candidates are qualified for selection for flight officer training programs. The exam is designed to test multiple different aspects of potential candidates, which is intended to be predictors of training performance. Some of the sections might not seem to have anything to do with actual aviation, but another goal of the exam is to determine overall academic ability and essentially how hard you are willing to work for it or not. In short: how smart are you and do you possess the drive and motivation required to be a leader in the US Army.

Sections on the SIFT

There are 7 sections on the SIFT as follows:

1. Simple Drawings (SD) – 2 minutes, 100 questions
2. Hidden Figures (HF) – 5 minutes, 50 questions
3. Army Aviation Information Test (AAIT) – 30 minutes, 40 questions
4. Spatial Apperception Test (SAT) – 10 minutes, 25 questions
5. Reading Comprehension Test (RCT)– 30 minutes, 20 questions
6. Math Skills Test (MST) – 40 minutes, test length varies
7. Mechanical Comprehension Test (MCT) – 15 minutes, test length varies

From the time you check-in for the exam, count on the entire exam lasting approximately 3 hours, although many test-takers often complete the exam in about 2 hours. We will cover each section in detail in the following chapters of this book, each followed up with practice questions like those you will see on the SIFT exam.

Scoring on the SIFT

Scores range from 20-80 with a 40 being a passing score. The low 50's is an average score. Obviously, you want to try to do better than that since the selection process is a competitive one, although there is varied reports of whether or not boards actually see your score or just that you passed without indicator of actual score. Either way, you should not treat test-day as a "trial run" and study hard now. You are only allowed take the SIFT twice in your life!

Additional Test Information

The most important sections to study for are those that lend themselves to be studied. Kind of a confusing statement, right? What is meant by that is of the 7 sections, you should devote a majority of your study time to three of them: Math Skills, Mechanical Comprehension, and Army Aviation Information. These sections will have the most bang for your buck for study effort, especially since many test-takers probably haven't studied math or physics (as found in the Mechanical Comprehension section) for many years, and very possibly have zero real-world experience with aviation.

The other 4 sections (Simple Drawings, Hidden Figures, Spatial Apperception, and Reading Comprehension) you need to familiarize yourself with and move on, as these sections you cannot "study" much beyond that. Your objective in preparation for these sections is just to make sure the first time you see them isn't on test day.

Overall, you should only spend a few hours in combined total studying for Simple Drawings, Hidden Figures, Spatial Apperception, and Reading Comprehension. Many will find they only spend 1 or 2 hours on them...maybe even less. The rest of your time should be devoted to the other three sections as they are more substantially more difficult, more academically driven (as opposed to "skills" like the other sections), cover more material, and will result in higher scores for your study effort.

Additional Resources

Keep in mind that while the SIFT is a relatively new test (introduced in 2013), many of the sections were picked up from the AFOQT for the Air Force and ASTB for the Naval forces. While the number of questions and time limits are different, you can find a plethora of practice tests and helpful information on discussion forums online.

Be certain to visit www.usarec.army.mil and find your way to the SIFT FAQ's...or just Google "SIFT exam" or "SIFT FAQ" and it will be the very first result. This is the official information about the SIFT exam and you should read it carefully.

Testing Strategies

There are two very different strategies you will have to utilize on the SIFT exam as there are two different types of subtest sections you will encounter.

The first are the "fixed number of questions" sections: Simple Drawings, Hidden Figures, Army Aviation Information Test, Spatial Apperception, and Reading Comprehension. On these sections, any question left unanswered is counted as incorrect, which simply means, don't leave a single question unanswered! If you see time is running out, guess on every question before the clock runs down. Also on these sections, you can go skip questions or go back later, so if time permits, check your work before moving on.

The second type of subtest is the "Computer Adaptive" type. This is only for the Math Skills and Mechanical Comprehension. Under no circumstances should you ever guess without first giving your very best effort on these sections. The reasons are two-fold: 1) you cannot go back and change answers later. 2) the "Adaptive" word means that each test is customized to each test taker. As you answer questions, depending on whether or not you answer them correctly or not will determine the question you get next. If you get a question right, the next question will be more difficult. If you get it wrong, the next one will be easier. Each time you get a wrong answer, you maximum possible score drops lower and lower. Blindly guessing will significantly decrease the possibility of even passing this section, because after too many wrong answers you essentially fail automatically. This is why the test lengths vary, because if you get 5 or 10 questions in row correct, they know you are good to go and you can move on. If you miss 5 or 10 in a row, they know you don't have a prayer of passing so don't bother giving you any more chances.

Chapter 1: Simple Drawings

As indicated in the name, this section is simple. So simple in fact, you should not spend more than about 10 minutes "studying" for this section. No, we are not kidding. In fact, most people will only need about 90 seconds. In fact, it isn't even really possible to "study", but only familiarize yourself with how this test section is designed and what you need to do.

You will have a mere 120 seconds to answer 100 questions in which you select a shape or object that is not like the other shape or objects. The questions are so simple however, that a pre-kindergartner could answer them. No, again, we aren't kidding. A 3 or 4 year old could answer these questions….maybe not necessarily as quickly as you can, but the point remains. As you noticed though, the trick is not in the difficulty (or lack thereof) of the questions themselves, but the fact that no one can possibly answer all 100 in the short amount of time allotted: 1.2 seconds per question.

The best way to prepare for this section is to just run through some practice questions. We gave you a quarter of the actual test length to see what it is like. Get a stop-watch or pull up a timer on your phone and go through all 25 as fast as possible without sacrificing accuracy. This will give you a rough idea of how many questions you will be able to answer on the actual test. Once you've done that….move on to the other sections!

You can theoretically "guess" on this test section if time is running out, but we advise against it. The better strategy in this instance is to just answer as many correctly as possible. Let's say you have 10 seconds left on the clock. You could just click "A" for every answer as fast as possible and get through 10 or maybe even 15 of them if you are lucky. You have a 20% chance (1 in 5) of answering correctly, so you would have statistically answered 2 or 3 correctly. Most test-takers typically are able to answer in the range of 70-85 questions in the Simple Drawings section. That means on average, it takes them 1.4 to 1.7 seconds per question. That means in the remaining 10 seconds, most people will be able to correct answer 5 to 7 more questions.

The bottom line? Try it out now and time yourself so you know what to expect on test day and have a ballpark of your speed in questions/second. On test day, do not even look at the clock. Each glance at the clock could eat up another potentially answered question.

Simple Drawings Practice Test

1.
   □   □   □   □   ■
   A.   B.   C.   D.   E.

2.
   =   =   =   =   ≥
   A.   B.   C.   D.   E.

3.
   ⊕   ⬤   ⬤   ⬤   ⬤
   A.   B.   C.   D.   E.

4.
   ⇧   ⇧   ⇧   ⬆   ⇧
   A.   B.   C.   D.   E.

5.
   A.   B.   C.   D.   E.

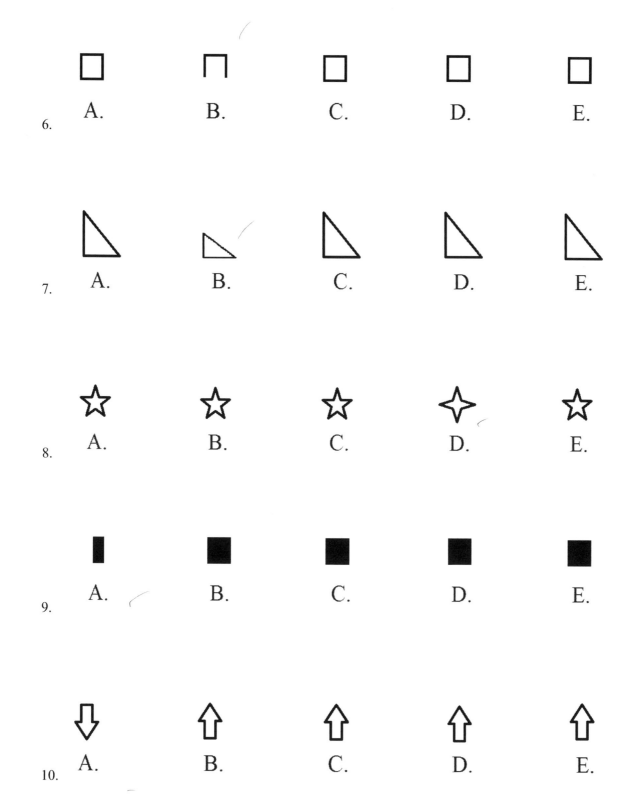

6. A.   B.   C.   D.   E.

7. A.   B.   C.   D.   E.

8. A.   B.   C.   D.   E.

9. A.   B.   C.   D.   E.

10. A.   B.   C.   D.   E.

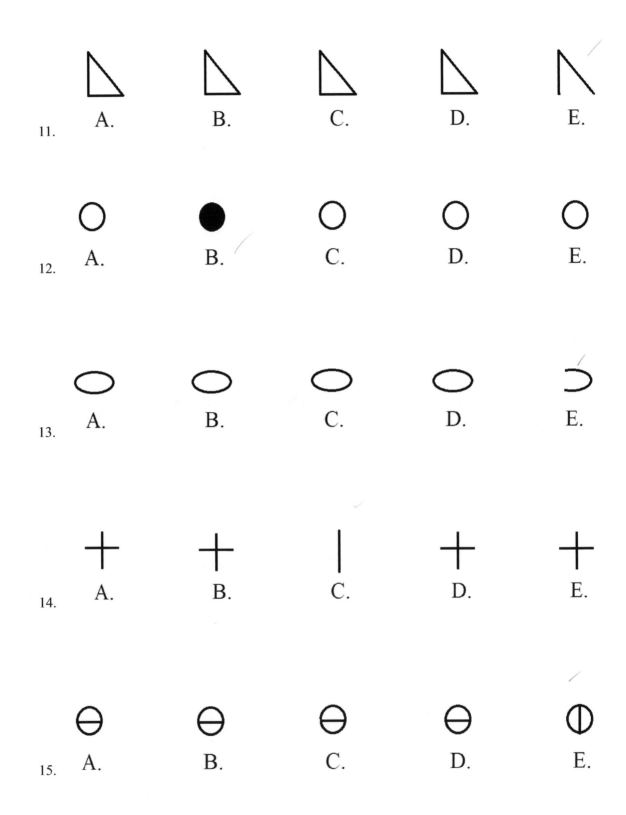

11.

   A.   B.   C.   D.   E.

12.

   A.   B.   C.   D.   E.

13.

   A.   B.   C.   D.   E.

14.

   A.   B.   C.   D.   E.

15.

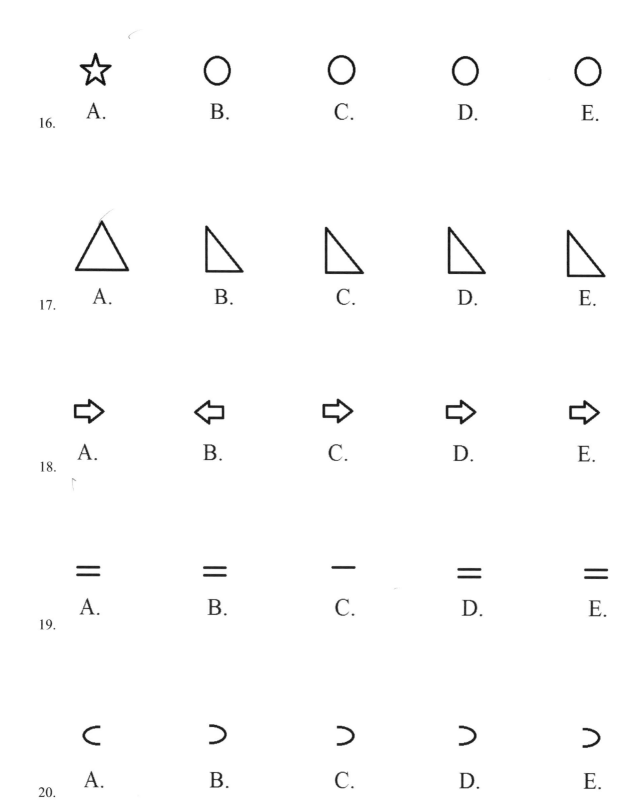

16.
A.   B.   C.   D.   E.

17.
A.   B.   C.   D.   E.

18.
A.   B.   C.   D.   E.

19.
A.   B.   C.   D.   E.

20.
A.   B.   C.   D.   E.

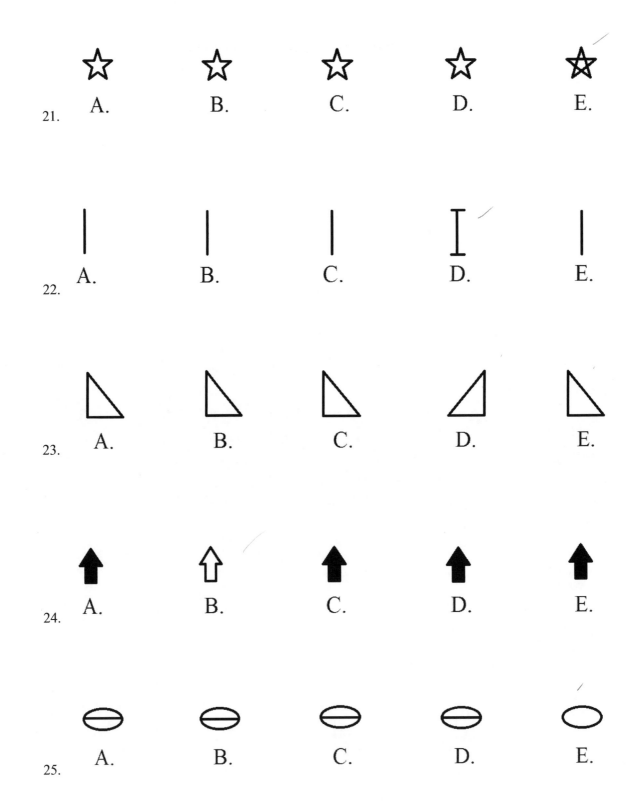

21. A.   B.   C.   D.   E.

22. A.   B.   C.   D.   E.

23. A.   B.   C.   D.   E.

24. A.   B.   C.   D.   E.

25. A.   B.   C.   D.   E.

Simple Drawings Practice Test – Answers

1. E
2. E
3. A
4. D
5. B
6. B
7. B
8. D
9. A
10. A
11. E
12. B
13. E
14. C
15. E
16. A
17. A
18. B
19. C
20. A
21. E
22. D
23. D
24. B
25. E

Chapter 2: Hidden Figures

In the hidden figures section, you will have 5 minutes to complete 50 items. The first thing you will notice about this section is the formatting of the questions is totally different than any other section. You will be given 5 shapes with correlating answer choices A, B, C, D, & E. Below those answer choices, you will be presented the questions which is a box with a lot of zig-zagging lines in all directions. Somewhere in those zig-zagged lines is a shape that matches one of the 5 answer choices.

This section is straightforward enough, but a few things to remember that can help you:

- First and foremost, it is imperative to remember that the shape in the hidden figure will always match the same size, position, and orientation as shown in the answer choice selections. Do not over-analyze and think you see a figure that is rotated 90 degrees or slightly bigger or smaller because the SIFT will never present questions that way on this section.
- Find a defining feature of the answer choices. That one long section or sharply angled protrusion can help you quickly ID the shape in many cases.
- Speed is essential here. You have 6 seconds per question, so you need to move through the questions with a purpose and never linger on a question for too long. That said, don't rush because the objective is to answer the questions correctly, not to see how fast you can click.
- Finally, this works for some and not for others…but if you squint and almost blur out the hidden figure image a little, sometimes the shapes will just kind of "appear" because there is a pattern to them, whereas the other lines in the box are just meant to distract and conceal. Not very scientific, we know, but this has been a life-saver for many people.

Let's get started with some practice on the next page. Do not let the hidden figure section overwhelm you. Even if you are struggling with it, just get familiar with how this section looks so you know what to expect on test day, but focus your attention on the other sections as they are more important, require more study time, and you will see more results from your study effort.

Hidden Figures Practice Test

For questions 1-5, use the below shapes as answer choices:

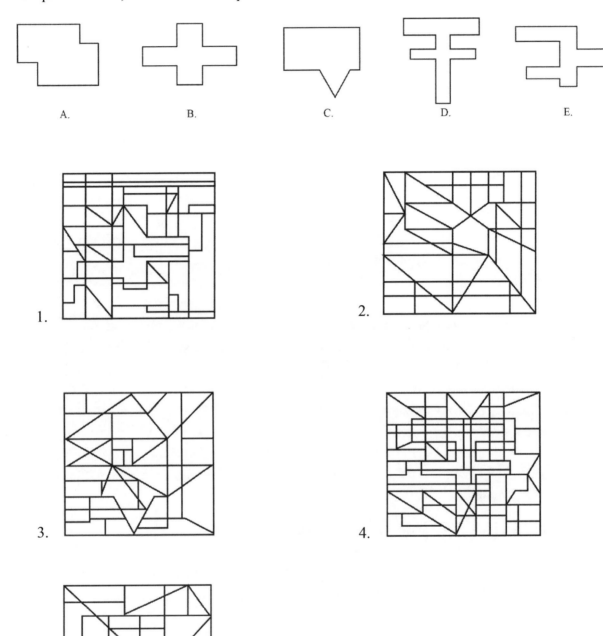

A. B. C. D. E.

1.

2.

3.

4.

5.

For questions 6-10, use the below shapes as answer choices:

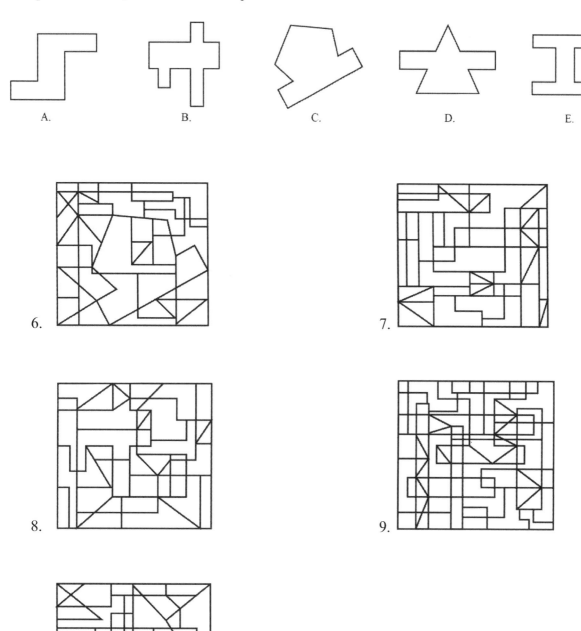

A.   B.   C.   D.   E.

6.

7.

8.

9.

10.

For questions 11-15, use the below shapes as answer choices:

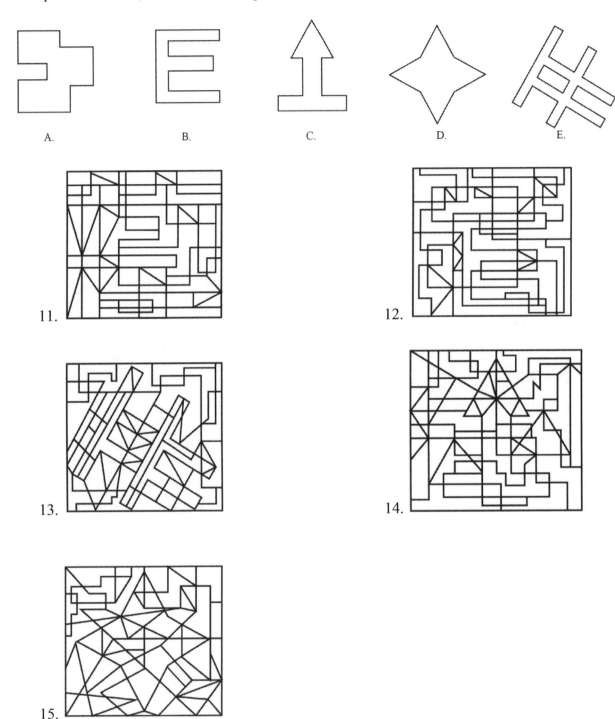

A.

B.

C.

D.

E.

11.

12.

13.

14.

15.

Hidden Figures Practice Test - Answers

1. E
2. B
3. C
4. D
5. A
6. C
7. A
8. B
9. E
10. D
11. A
12. B
13. E
14. C
15. D

Chapter 3: Army Aviation Information Test

The Army Aviation Information Test (AAIT) allows for 30 minutes to answer 40 multiple choice questions about aviation and helicopters in specific. If you have aviation experience such as private pilot's license, you are ahead of the curve but will still need to do some in depth studying as much of this information is technical and not so much about actually flying a plane. Unless you consider yourself an aviation expert already, you will need to study regardless of your current capability. Even those with PPL's report that this section was tough and required substantial studying effort.

A lot of information about helicopters is online. For example, the website of the Federal Aviation Administration (faa.gov) includes a 198-page, downloadable document, "Helicopter Flying Handbook." It is extremely important to download this resource and study it in depth. YouTube also has instructional videos about helicopters that can be quite helpful to better visualize and understand the concepts needed for this section.

Helicopter structure and components

During the past century, there have been many rotary-wing aircraft designed and built, including more than 400 types of helicopters. A helicopter is a type of rotorcraft that is able to takeoff and land vertically, hover, and fly forward, backward, and side to side (laterally). It can do so because it is equipped with a source of thrust: an engine that produces power and delivers it to overhead and tail rotors (on most helicopters) via one or more transmissions and drive shafts.

Helicopter engines are either piston or turbine; the advantage of the latter over the former is more thrust per pound.

Looking at a helicopter, we see a main body (fuselage) with a shaft (mast) protruding from the top. On the upper part of the fuselage of many helicopters is a cowling (shaped metal skin) that covers the aircraft's engine and transmission. Some helicopters have the engines externally mounted.

Depending on the type of helicopter, between two and six rotor blades are attached to the mast via a rotor head, which consists of several components, including a stabilizer bar (also called a flybar). The main rotor involves a complex swashplate mechanical system, which translate inputs from the pilot via the helicopter's flight controls into blade movement. Rotor system components include upper and lower swashplates, blade grips, control rods, pitch and scissor links, teeter or coning hinges, pitch horns, and counterweights.

The flybar's function is to enhance flight stability by keeping the bar stable as the rotor spins, and to reduce crosswind thrust on the blades. Through mechanical linkages, the bar's rotation combines with the swashplate's movement to damp internal (steering) and external (wind) forces on the rotor. The mechanical device makes it easier for the pilot to control the helicopter.

To provide additional stability, many helicopters have a horizontal stabilizer located roughly half way along the tail boom. The stabilizer helps to level the aircraft during forward flight.

Aft of the fuselage is a tail boom, which contains a drive shaft for the tail rotor, which is installed on the fin at the end of the helicopter. Tail rotors have two or more blades, depending on the size of the aircraft. They spin in the vertical plane, while the main, overhead rotor spins in an adjustable horizontal plane.

Some tail rotor tips are covered by a shroud made of formed metal or another durable material. The assembly is known as a ducted fan and the design reduces the possibility of someone walking into the spinning rotor blades and being injured or killed. The U.S. Coast Guard's Eurocopter HH-65 Dolphin is an example of a ducted fan helicopter.

Attached to the underside of many types of helicopters are a pair of skids that parallel the aircraft's longitudinal (nose-to-tail) axis. Some rotary-wing aircraft such as the U.S. Army's AH-64 Apache helicopter have wheels that hang down below the fuselage to absorb the weight of the aircraft when it is on the ground. Other helicopters have retractable wheels (called landing gear).

In a helicopter's cockpit are the pilots' seats, flight instruments and controls (cyclic, collective, throttle, and pedals), avionics (electronics used for navigation, communications, and aircraft systems), weapons controls (in military helicopters), and other equipment (e.g., fire extinguisher, flashlight).

Aerodynamics forces

There are four main aerodynamic forces that act on a helicopter when it is airborne: weight, lift, thrust, and drag.

Everything on a helicopter – the aircraft's structure and components, pilots, fuel, cargo, etc. – has *weight*. Because of the earth's gravitational pull, the combined mass of a helicopter and its contents acts downward. From a physics perspective, the total weight force is deemed to act through a helicopter's center of gravity.

Aerodynamic loads associated with flight maneuvers and air turbulence affect the aircraft's weight. Whenever a helicopter flies a curved flight path at a certain altitude, the load factor (force of gravity, or "G") exerted on the rotor blades is greater than the aircraft's total weight.

When a pilot turns a helicopter by banking it, the amount of "G" increases. Banking more in order to turn more tightly causes the aircraft's weight to increase further. A helicopter banked 30 degrees weighs an additional 16 percent, but at 60 degrees of bank – a very steep turn – the aircraft weighs twice as much as it does in straight and level flight in smooth air.

Gusts produced by turbulent air can suddenly increase the angle of attack (AOA) of the rotor blades, which enlarges the load factor acting on them.

Lift is the force that counteracts an aircraft's weight and causes a helicopter to rise into the air and stay aloft. Lift is produced by airfoils – rotor blades, in the case of helicopters – that move through the air at a speed sufficient to create a pressure differential between the two sides of the airfoils. Lift acts perpendicular to the direction of flight through the airfoil's center of pressure, or center of lift.

Thrust is an aircraft's forward force, which is created by one or more engines (there are three in some rotary-wing machines), and is transformed in the case of helicopters into rotary motion via the components mentioned (transmission, drive shafts, rotor head, blades). Generally, thrust acts parallel to the aircraft's longitudinal axis, but not always.

Drag opposes thrust; it is a rearward-acting force caused by airflow passing over the aircraft's structure and becoming disrupted. Drag acts parallel to the relative wind. There are three types of drag that act on aircraft: profile, induced, and parasite.

As the main and tail rotors spin and the helicopter accelerates, *profile drag* created by the blades' frictional resistance increases. Profile drag consists of skin friction created by surface imperfections and form drag; the latter is caused by wake turbulence, airflow separating from the surface of an aircraft structure and creating eddies. The amount of form drag is a function of the size and shape of the structure as it protrudes into the relative wind.

Induced drag is created by air circulating around each rotor blade as it spins and creates lift; the circulation causes a vortex behind each blade. There is also a downward deflection of the airstream. As more lift is produced, induced drag and rotor downwash both increase. As well, increasing the AOA of the rotor blades, a technique used to increase lift, results in stronger vortices and greater induced drag. Because helicopters need a lot of lift, particularly at low speeds and while hovering, a high AOA during takeoff and initial climb and final approach and landing results in the greatest induced drag. Conversely, at cruising airspeeds when the rotor blades' AOA is shallow, induced drag is relatively small.

Parasite drag is created by helicopter components and attached equipment that do not contribute to lift, including the fuselage and tail section, skids or wheels, externally mounted engines, sensors, and weapons. These structures create a loss of airstream momentum proportional to their size and greater parasite drag at higher airspeeds. In fact, parasite drag varies with the square of the aircraft's velocity, so doubling the airspeed quadruples this type of drag.

A helicopter's *total drag*, which can be plotted on a graph as a curve, with airspeed on the other axis, is the sum of its profile, induced, and parasite drag. The curve's low point is the intersection of a certain airspeed and the smallest total drag. In other words, it is the point where the helicopter's lift-to-drag ratio (L/DMAX) is the greatest. At this speed, the total lift capacity is maximized, an aspect of helicopter performance of singular importance to pilots.

Relevant scientific principles

Bernoulli's Principle
In 1738, a Swiss scientist named Daniel Bernoulli published a book entitled *Hydrodynamica* in which he explained that an increase of the inviscid flow of a fluid (i.e., the flow of an ideal, zero-viscosity liquid or gas) resulted in a decrease of fluid pressure. Bernoulli's famous equation is $P + \frac{1}{2}\rho v^2 = $ a constant, where P = pressure (a force exerted divided by the area exerted upon); ρ (the Greek letter "rho") = the fluid's density; and v = the fluid's velocity.

The constant in Bernoulli's formula is derived from the scientific principle that energy cannot be created or destroyed – only its form can be changed – and a system's total energy does not increase or decrease.

Conservation of energy
Bernoulli's Principle is based on the conservation of energy, which says that in a steady flow the sum of all forms of mechanical energy – a fluid's potential energy plus its kinetic energy – along a streamline (e.g., a tube) is the same at all points. Thus, greater fluid flow rate (higher speed) results in increased kinetic energy and dynamic pressure and reduced potential energy and static pressure.

A helicopter filled with fuel has a finite amount of energy. Through combustion in the engine, the fuel's heat energy is converted to kinetic energy through the transmission. If a helicopter were to be airborne when it ran out of fuel, the only energy left would be potential energy, a function of the aircraft's height above the ground. As the pilot nosed the helicopter down in order to keep air flowing over the rotor blades, a maneuver called autorotation, the aircraft's potential energy would be converted into kinetic energy.

Combining Bernoulli's Principle with the fact that helicopters have blades (airfoils) that spin and provide lift at varying speeds during different phases of flight (takeoff, climb, cruise, descent, landing), the lift produced in a given instant can be calculated using the following equation: $L = \frac{1}{2}\rho v^2 A C_l$, where L = the lift force, $\frac{1}{2}\rho v2$ was previously explained, A = the airfoil's area (length multiplied by width), and C_l is the coefficient of lift of the rotor blades.

Pilots must remember that the lifting force on their aircraft is proportional to the density (ρ) of air through which they fly (higher altitude = less dense air), the aircraft's speed, and airfoil AOA.

Venturi Effect
To understand how spinning rotor blades can produce enough force to lift a helicopter off the ground, climb, and maintain a cruising altitude, and how a moving tail rotor is able to

generate a sideways, anti-torque force, we need to examine a phenomenon called the Venturi Effect.

In the late 18th century, an Italian physicist, Giovanni Battista Venturi, conducted experiments with a pump and an unusual tube. The diameter of one end of the tube was constant, while the circumference of the tube's central portion was smaller. Downstream from the bottleneck, the tube's diameter increased. It was as though someone had squeezed the center of the tube, creating a constriction.

Venturi noticed that as fluids moved through the tube, the flow rate increased (accelerated) and the force (static pressure) against the tube's surface decreased as the diameter became smaller. The opposite also happened: increasing tube diameter downstream resulted in reduced flow rate (deceleration) and greater static pressure. Venturi published his findings in 1797 and the effect that he observed, measured, and wrote about became associated with his name. It has certainly been integral to aviation since the development of gliding in the 19th century.

If a Venturi tube is cut in half longitudinally, the curvature of the tube wall would look similar to that of the top of a helicopter's rotor blade or an airplane's wing, which is also an airfoil. When a helicopter rotor blade spins, it "slices" the air, forcing molecules to travel along one side of the airfoil or the other. Those moving across the curved side have to travel a greater distance to reach the trailing edge than those moving across the relatively flat side. Consequently, the air molecules moving across the curved surface accelerate, as they did in Venturi's tube, and the static pressure drops.

Because pressure flows from high to low, the static pressure differential experienced between the two sides of rotating helicopter blades results in a force exerted on each airfoil from the high-pressure (flat) side to the low-pressure (curved) surface. In this way, lift is generated by the main rotor, and an anti-torque force acting perpendicular to the helicopter's longitudinal axis is created by the tail rotor (a smaller version of the overhead rotor turned vertically, essentially).

Newton's Third Law of Motion
Sir Isaac Newton (1642–1727) was a brilliant English physicist and mathematician who formulated universal laws of motion, including his third, which stated: "When one body exerts a force on a second body, the second body simultaneously exerts a force equal in magnitude and opposite in direction to that of the first body."

Rotor blades on helicopters designed and built in the United States, Canada, Britain, and Germany move in a counter-clockwise direction when viewed from above, and clockwise on rotary-wing aircraft made in Russia and other countries. Because of Newton's Third Law of Motion, the torque effect of the spinning main rotor is to rotate the aircraft in the opposite direction. To prevent this undesirable rotation, a sideways, anti-torque force is created on most helicopters by the spinning a tail rotor.

Alternatively, to eliminate torque counter-rotating rotors are used on other types of helicopters. Examples include the Boeing CH-47 Chinook (tandem rotors), Kaman K-1200 K-MAX (intermeshing rotors), and Kamov Ka-50 "Black Shark" (coaxial rotors).

Flight controls

As mentioned, a helicopter has four controls that allow the pilot to maneuver the aircraft: the cyclic, collective, throttle, and pedals.

The *cyclic* control, which is typically called the "cyclic" or "cyclic stick", is located in front of the pilot(s) in the cockpit. It is similar to a joystick used to play video games in that it moves in all directions except up and down. By moving the control, the pilot varies the pitch of the main rotor blades on a cyclical basis (i.e., every revolution) via the complex rotor head system. The rotor head has been designed so that all blades have the same angle of incidence (explained later) at the same point during each revolution (cycle).

Moving the cyclic results in a change of blade angle of attack, thus generating variable lift as each blade spins around the mast. Blades rise or fall in sequence due to increasing or decreasing AOA. For example, if the pilot moves the cyclic forward, the aft part of the rotor disk rises because of greater aft blade AOA, while the front drops. The result is a forward-tilting disk and a corresponding thrust vector imparted to the helicopter, which moves forward.

The *collective* is on the left side of the pilot's seat, moves up and down, and can be adjusted in terms of its position via a variable friction lock to prevent unwanted movement. Adjusting the collective alters the AOA of all the main rotor blades simultaneously, irrespective of their position. Pulling up on the collective increases blade AOA and aircraft climb rate; lowering it has the opposite effect.

In many helicopters, the *throttle*, which controls the power produced by the engine and rotates like a motorcycle throttle, is located at the end of the collective. In some turbine helicopters, the throttle control is mounted on the cockpit floor or an overhead panel. Single-engine helicopters typically have the motorcycle-style twist grip, while helicopters with two or more powerplants have a throttle lever for each engine.

Helicopter anti-torque *pedals* are located on the floor in front of the pilot(s) and used to control yaw (i.e., where the aircraft is pointing). Stepping on the left or right pedal causes the AOA of the tail rotor blades to change accordingly, altering the horizontal thrust vector created by the aft spinning airfoils. Viewed from above, the amount of horizontal "lift" (the sideways-acting force) generated by the tail rotor increases or decreases with pedal movement, changing the turning moment (force) acting on the helicopter in opposition to the torque force previously explained. As the tail moves left or right, the aircraft's nose moves in the opposite direction. When the pilot wants the helicopter's nose to move left or right, he or she pushes on the corresponding pedal.

Additional helicopter terms, definitions, and explanations (in alphabetical order)

Advancing blade: As the main rotor spins, with each revolution the blades move either toward the front of the helicopter or its tail. In the case of the former, each blade advances, and doing so increases the relative wind speed across the airfoil. Consequently, lift increases and the blade moves (flaps) upward.

Airflow in forward flight: When a helicopter flies forward, air flows in a direction opposite to that of the aircraft, with a speed equal to the machine's forward velocity. Because the rotor spins, the speed of air flowing across each blade depends on the airfoil's position in the plane of rotation and the helicopter's airspeed. With each revolution, the longitudinal velocity vector of each blade is sometimes with the aircraft's forward speed and sometimes against it.

Consequently, the airflow meeting each blade varies as a function of its position in the circular movement cycle. For helicopters with a main rotor that spins counter-clockwise, the maximum airflow speed happens when the blade reaches the three o'clock (right) position. As the blade passes over the aircraft's forward fuselage and nose, the speed decreases. The lowest airflow velocity happens when the blade reaches the nine o'clock (left) position. As the blade crosses the helicopter's tail, airflow speed increases to rotor spin (rotational) velocity and then accelerates as the blade moves toward the right side.

Airfoil: An airfoil is a surface that generates lift greater than drag as air flows over the upper and lower surfaces. Helicopter main rotor and tail rotor blades are examples of airfoils, as is the horizontal stabilizer. Airfoils are carefully designed and can be made of non-metallic materials such as composites.

Angle of attack: The angle between the chord line of an airfoil (e.g., a rotor blade) and the airfoil's direction of motion relative to the air (the relative wind). AOA is an aerodynamic angle.

Angle of incidence: The angle between the chord line of each blade and the rotor system's plane of rotation (e.g., level, tilted). AOI is a mechanical angle.

Autorotation: A situation where the main rotor generates lift not because of a functioning engine, but solely because air flows across the blades is called autorotation. When a helicopter engine fails, a clutch mechanism called a freewheeling unit automatically disconnects the engine from the main rotor, allowing the latter to spin freely. During autorotation, the helicopter descends, causing air to flow across the blades and continuing to provide lift as they spin in the airstream.

Learning to perform an autorotation to a successful landing is an important part of helicopter pilot training and must be demonstrated to an inspector in order to obtain the desired certification. To be certified with civil or military aviation authorities, helicopters must have a freewheeling unit that allows for autorotation.

Autorotation (during forward flight): During an autorotation when the helicopter is moving forward, the rotor disk takes in upward flowing air and the driven, driving, and stall regions of each blade move outboard along its length (span), but only on the retreating side of the disk. With a lower AOA on the advancing blade, the driven region expands, while on the retreating blade, the stall region enlarges. Also, reversed airflow occurs in a small section near the root of the retreating blade, reducing the driven region.

Autorotation (while hovering): During an autorotation in a hover (in still air), dissymmetry of lift due to helicopter speed is not a factor because the forces that cause the blades to spin are similar for all the airfoils, regardless of whether they are advancing or retreating. The force vectors acting in the driven, driving, and stall regions of each blade are different because the rotational relative wind is slower near the blade root and greater toward the blade tip. Also, there is a smaller AOA in the driven region compared to the driving region due to blade twist. Inflow of air up through the rotor combined with the rotational relative wind creates varying aerodynamic forces at every point along the blade.

In the driven region during an autorotation while hovering, some lift is produced, but it is offset by drag due to the total aerodynamic force (TAF) acting aft of the axis of rotation. The net result is rotor deceleration. The size of the driven region varies with the number of rotor revolutions per minute (rpm), blade pitch, and the rate of descent.

TAF in the driving region – also called the autorotative region – is angled slightly forward of the axis of rotation, resulting in an acceleration force that provides thrust and a blade rotation acceleration tendency. Rotor rpm, blade pitch, and rate of descent affect the driving region's size, which the pilot can control, thereby altering autorotative rpm.

The inner one-quarter of the rotor blade is the stall region and operates above the stall angle (the maximum AOA) during an autorotation while hovering. In this part of the rotor disk, drag is created that reduces blade rotation.

Blade flapping: Too much lift causes blade flapping. In a hover, the blade angle is such that lift and centrifugal forces balance out. However, if lift is increased (due to excessive airspeed of the advancing blades) and centrifugal force remains unchanged, the extra lift will cause the blade to move upward to a point where the lift and centrifugal forces are again in balance.

Blade span: The distance from the tip of the rotor blade to the center of the drive shaft (rotational center point).

Blade twist: Greater pitch angles toward the blade root where rotational velocity is relatively low and progressively shallower pitch angles toward the blade tip where rotational velocity is comparatively high describes the design feature known as blade twist. Its purpose is to distribute the lifting force more evenly along the airfoil, thereby smoothing out internal blade stresses.

Chord: The distance between the leading and trailing edges along the chord line is an airfoil's chord. If the blade is tapered, as viewed from above or below, the chord at its tip will be different than at its root. Average chord describes the average distance.

Chord line: An imaginary straight line from the airfoil's leading (front) edge to its trailing (aft) edge.

Coning: A spinning rotor creates centrifugal force (inertia) that pulls the blades outward from the hub. The inertia is proportional to the rotational speed. As the rotating blades produce lift – during takeoff, for example – centrifugal force combines with the upward lift force to create a slightly conical shape (when the rotor is viewed from the side).

Coning angle: The angle formed between spinning rotor blades and a plane perpendicular to the mast.

Coriolis Effect (Law of Conservation of Angular Momentum): The Coriolis Effect states that a rotating body spins at the same speed (angular momentum) unless an external force is applied to change the rotational velocity. Angular momentum is the rotational speed multiplied by the moment of inertia (mass times distance from the center of rotation squared). Also, angular acceleration and deceleration occurs as a spinning body's mass is moved closer to or farther away from the axis of rotation, respectively. The speed of the rotating mass changes proportionately with the square of the radius (the distance between the spinning body and the center of rotation).

In the context of helicopters, as coning occurs the rotor's diameter decreases. However, due to the law of conservation of angular momentum the blades' speed remains the same despite the fact that the tips now travel a shorter distance due to the smaller disk diameter. What changes is rotor rpm, which increases lift slightly.

Dissymmetry of lift: Different wind flow speeds across the advancing and retreating halves of the rotor disk result in a dissymmetry of lift. After a helicopter takes off, the relative wind speed experienced by the advancing blade is increased by the aircraft's forward speed, while the opposite occurs on the retreating blade (due to the machine's forward vector). Consequently, the advancing side of the rotor disk produces more lift than the retreating blade side.

Left uncorrected, this situation would cause the helicopter to become uncontrollable. To eliminate dissymmetry of lift, the main rotor blades flap and rotate automatically with each revolution. A semi-rigid rotor system (comprised of two blades, as is common on light helicopters) involves a teetering hinge, which allows the blades to flap as a unit; when one blade flaps down, the other blade flaps up. Rotor systems with three or more blades use a horizontal flapping hinge, which permits each blade to flap up and down as it rotates around the mast.

Driven region: Also called the propeller region, the driven region is nearest to the blade tips and normally consists of nearly one-third (30 percent) of the radius. The driven region tends to slow the rotor's spin due to drag resulting from the region's TAF, which is inclined slightly behind the axis of rotation.

Driving region: Also known as the autorotative region, the driving region is normally between a blade's driven and stall regions. The total aerodynamic force of the driving region is inclined slightly forward of the axis of rotation, supplying thrust and accelerating the blade's rotation.

Effective translational lift (ETL): Helicopters experience effective translational lift while transitioning to forward flight at about 16 to 24 knots. By the upper end of the speed range, the aircraft has managed to out-run the blade vortices created during takeoff and initial forward acceleration. During ETL, the rotor system begins to pass through air that is relatively undisturbed and the airflow becomes more horizontal, resulting in less downwash and induced drag. Also, efficiency of the rotor system and helicopter airspeed both increase during ETL and the machine accelerates toward the part of flight where L/DMAX occurs.

As the airspeed increases and translational lift becomes more effective, the aircraft's nose pitches up and the helicopter rolls to the right (with a rotor system spinning counter-clockwise), movements that must be corrected by the pilot. The machine's tendency to behave this way during ETL is the result of dissymmetry of lift, gyroscopic precession, and transverse flow effect. Once the helicopter has transitioned through ETL, the pilot must push forward and left on the cyclic to maintain a constant attitude of the rotor disk.

Forward flight: In steady forward flight, lift is offset by weight and the forces of thrust and drag are equal. When the tip-path (rotation) plane is tilted forward (due to the pilot pushing the cyclic forward), the total lift-thrust force, which consists of horizontal and vertical components, is also angled forward. Because of these horizontal components, as the helicopter moves forward it begins to lose altitude (due to the reduced vertical lift vector), a situation the pilot must correct.

As the helicopter begins to accelerate from a hover, translational lift causes the efficiency of the rotor system to increase, resulting in power in excess of that which was needed for hovering. Continued acceleration increases airflow and expands the excess power. Once the helicopter has reached its assigned or desired altitude and airspeed, the pilot reduces the power to maintain straight-and-level, unaccelerated flight, noting the torque (power) setting and not making any major changes to the flight controls.

Gyroscopic precession: When a force is applied to a spinning mass (e.g., a child's top, a helicopter rotor), the resulting effect occurs not at the point of force application, but 90 degrees later in the direction of rotation. In a helicopter, if a downward force is applied, say, on the starboard (right) side of the counter-clockwise-spinning rotor disk, the movement response occurs at the rotor's twelve o'clock position (i.e., in front of the fuselage). Wind gusts can apply such forces on rotors.

Hovering flight: One element of vertical flight is hovering. To hover a helicopter, the main rotor must produce lift equal to the aircraft's total weight. At high rotor rpm and increasing blade pitch (AOA) generate the lift required to hover. During hovering, rotor blade tip vortices reduce the effectiveness of the outer blade and negatively affect the lift of the following blades. For this reason, a lot of power is required during a hover.

Because of the helicopter's blade downwash (induced flow) while it is hovering, the velocity of air under the aircraft can reach 60 to 100 knots, depending on the rotor's diameter and the machine's size and weight.

During the hover, the relative wind and AOA are changed by the downward airflow and the TAF is reduced. Consequently, the pilot has to increase collective pitch (pull up on the collective) to create enough TAF to continue hovering. However, the increase in lift is accompanied by greater induced drag, so the total power needed to hover is greater, requiring the pilot to increase the engine throttle.

Induced flow (downwash): As rotor blades spin, they create rotational relative wind, airflow that is parallel as well as opposite to the rotor's plane of rotation and perpendicular to each blade's leading edge. As the blades rotate, air accelerates over the airfoils and is projected downward. Moving a large amount of air vertically and down through the rotor system, which occurs during takeoff and hover, creates induced flow, which can greatly alter the efficiency of the system. Rotational relative wind combines with downwash to form a resultant relative wind, which becomes more vertical as induced flow increases.

In ground effect (IGE): A "cushion" of air beneath moving airfoils (e.g., spinning rotor blades) and the takeoff/landing surface (e.g., a heliport deck) provides additional lift to the aircraft when it is close to the ground. During IGE, lift acts more vertically, induced drag is reduced, and the relative wind is more horizontal, all of which increases the efficiency of the rotor system. Maximum ground effect occurs during a hover above smooth, hard surfaces, up to a height equal to the main rotor's diameter.

Inherent sideslip: In forward flight, the tail rotor creates a sideward force and the helicopter slightly tilts to the wind when the main rotor disk is level and the slip ball in the pilot's turn-and-bank indicator is centered. The fin (vertical stabilizer) on larger helicopters is designed with the tail rotor mounted in such a way as to correct inherent sideslip. Also, installing the tail rotor on top of the fin places the anti-torque force vector closer to the horizontal plane of the main rotor's torque, reducing tilt when the aircraft is airborne.

Mean camber line: An imaginary line between the leading and trailing edges and halfway between the airfoil's upper (curved) and lower (relatively flat) surfaces.

Non-symmetrical airfoil (cambered): When one surface of an airfoil has a specific curvature that the opposite side does not, the airfoil is described as non-symmetrical, or cambered. The advantage of a non-symmetrical helicopter blade, for example, is that it produces lift at an AOA of zero degrees (as long as airflow is moving past the blade). Moreover, the lift-to-drag ratio and stall characteristics of a cambered airfoil are better than those of a symmetrical airfoil. Its disadvantages are center of the pressure movement chord-wise by as much as one-fifth the chord line distance, which causes undesirable blade torsion, and greater airfoil production costs.

Out of ground effect (OGE): Once a helicopter climbs to an altitude that exceeds the diameter of the main rotor, it is said to be out of ground effect. The IGE air "cushion" is gone and because the horizontal component of the relative wind decreases while induced drag increases, there is a decrease in lift. A greater blade angle is needed to maintain lift, but increasing the blade pitch also creates more drag. For this reason, increasing pitch while hovering in OGE requires more power than during an IGE hover. Also, under certain conditions there is a localized downward airflow that causes the helicopter to sink at an alarming rate, an effect called settling with power.

Pendular action: In terms of physics, a helicopter with a single main rotor is suspended from a single point in space and swings like a pendulum. Since a pilot can exacerbate pendular action by over-controlling the aircraft, he or she needs to fly using smooth control inputs.

Rearward flight: When the rotor disc is tilted rearward, flight in that direction occurs. In such a situation, the pilot must be mindful that the vertical component of the drag vector acts in the same direction as lift (up) and weight (down). Because the horizontal stabilizer on the tail boom is designed to function during forward, not rearward flight, when the latter occurs the likelihood of the tail skid striking the ground (at a very low altitude) increases. Also, with the pilot seated facing forward and the helicopter's skids (if so equipped) not curved upward on the aft end, rearward flight hazards are greater than when flying forward.

Relative wind: The flow of air in relation to a helicopter's blades is called the relative wind. It moves in a direction opposite to that of the aircraft and spinning rotor. Rotating helicopter blades experience a relative wind comprised of horizontal and vertical parts, the former resulting from the turning blades plus the aircraft's movement through the air, and the latter due to induced flow plus air movement as the helicopter climbs or descends.

Resultant relative wind: Airflow created by the rotor's spin and modified by induced flow (downwash) creates the resultant relative wind. When the helicopter is moving horizontally, the resultant relative wind changes with the aircraft's speed. The airspeed component of the relative wind is added to the rotational relative wind when the blade is advancing, and subtracted when the blade is retreating.

Retreating blade stall: As the helicopter's forward speed increases, the airspeed of the retreating blade decreases. However, to ensure aircraft flight stability the retreating blade needs to produce as much lift as the advancing blade. Therefore, the AOA of the retreating blade must be increased to augment lift in the retreating portion of the rotor disk. If the helicopter's forward speed reaches a value that exceeds the velocity associated with the maximum AOA of the retreating blade, it will stall (i.e., no longer generate lift).

When a rotor blade enters a stall, the pilot feels an abnormal vibration due to the loss of lift. A deepening stall results in the aircraft rolling and pitching nose up.
A blade stall is caused by high blade loading (due to high helicopter gross weight), low rotor rpm, operating at a high density altitude, steep or abrupt turns, and/or turbulent air.

With the onset of rotor blade stall, corrective action taken by the pilot involves reducing power (by lowering the collective), airspeed, and "G" loads during maneuvering; increasing rotor rpm to the maximum permitted; and checking pedal trim.

Rotational relative wind (tip-path plane): As rotor blades spin, they produce a rotational relative wind, as called tip-path plane. Rotational relative wind, which strikes a blade perpendicular to its leading edge and parallel to the plane of rotation, constantly changes as the rotor spins. The wind velocity is greatest at the tip of each blade and decreases to zero at the mast's center.

Rotor blade angles: Two rotor blade angles are key aspects of helicopter aerodynamics: angle of attack and angle of incidence.

Rotor system: A helicopter's rotor system consists of the following main components:

- Hub: the mechanical apparatus on the upper mast where the root of each rotor blade is installed.
- Tip: the rotor blade section farthest from the hub.
- Root: the part of the blade where it is attached to the hub.
- Twist: the change in angle designed and built into the blade from the root to the tip.

Settling with power: Also known as vortex ring state, settling with power occurs when a helicopter sinks into its own downwash. Settling with power involves a descent straight down or nearly vertical at a minimum of 300 feet per minute and low forward speed. As well, the main rotor system must be using between 20 and 100 percent of engine power, leaving – in some cases – insufficient power for the pilot to stop the sink rate.

Vortex ring state can occur during approaches with a tailwind or when there is turbulence caused by one or more nearby helicopters, as has happened during formation approaches.

Settling with power also creates a secondary vortex ring around each blade's point where airflow changes from up to down. The net result is turbulence over a considerable portion of the spinning blades, which causes a reduction of rotor efficiency despite the fact that the engine is still delivering power to the system.

Sideward flight: For a helicopter to fly sideways, the main rotor disc must be tilted in the desired direction, causing a sideways component of the lift vector to be generated and take effect on the aircraft. Because of parasite drag caused by the helicopter moving sideways through the air and the lack of a horizontal stabilizer for such movement, sideward flight can create a very unstable condition. The pilot needs to be aware of any obstruction to the left or right of the helicopter and bear in mind the relatively low position of the rotor disk edge at the three or nine o'clock position during sideward flight.

Stall region: The inboard one-quarter of the rotor blade is known as the stall region, which operates above the stall angle of attack and creates drag. The stall region tends to slow down the spinning rotor.

Symmetrical airfoil: When an airfoil has identical upper and lower surfaces, it is symmetrical and produces no lift at an AOA of zero degrees. The main rotor blades of most light helicopters are symmetrical.

Total aerodynamic force (TAF): Two components comprise the total aerodynamic force: lift and drag. The amount of lift and drag produced by an airfoil are primarily determined by its shape and area.

Translational lift: Enhanced rotor efficiency due to the helicopter transitioning from a hover to directional flight results in translational lift. The relative wind increases during directional flight acceleration, augmenting airflow across the rotor blades while the turbulence and vortices associated with hovering decrease.

Translating tendency (drift): A helicopter with one main rotor tends to drift in the direction of tail rotor thrust (i.e., laterally). The following features have been incorporated into helicopters (with a main rotor that spins counter-clockwise) to counteract the drifting tendency:

1. Tilting the rotor mast to the left (as viewed from behind the helicopter), which is accomplished by doing the same to the main transmission. The mast tilt opposes the tail rotor thrust responsible for the translating tendency.
2. Rigging the flight controls so that the main rotor disk is tilted slightly left when the cyclic is centered.

Translational thrust: While transitioning from hover to forward flight, relative wind flows across the tail rotor, increasing its aerodynamic efficiency, a phenomenon called translational thrust. As the tail rotor becomes more aerodynamically efficient, it produces greater anti-torque thrust, which results in the helicopter's nose yawing left (in a helicopter with a main rotor spinning counter-clockwise). To counteract the yaw, the pilot applies right pedal, decreasing the tail rotor blades' AOA.

Transverse flow effect: When accelerating in forward flight, induced flow (downwash) at the forward disk area decreases, while increasing in the aft disk area. The difference between the two rotor regions is called transverse flow effect. Because of the effect as well as gyroscopic precession, acceleration through about 20 knots or into a 20-knot headwind causes the helicopter (with a rotor that spins counter-clockwise) to roll to the right. Transverse flow effect is countered by the pilot moving the cyclic to the left.

36

Turning flight: In a banking turn, the rotor disk is tilted by movement of the cyclic to the left or right side, an action that creates a sideway component of the lift vector. This horizontal force – called the centripetal force – opposes inertia, or centrifugal force. As the bank angle increases, the centripetal force becomes greater, causing the turn rate to increase. However, the vertical component of the lift vector decreases. To compensate and maintain altitude, the pilot must enlarge the blades' AOA by increasing (pulling up on) the collective.

Vertical flight: To achieve vertical flight upward, the helicopter's lift and thrust must exceed its weight and drag. Increasing the main rotor blades' AOA while maintaining their rotational speed creates extra lift and the aircraft ascends. Decreasing the pitch results in a descent.

Vortex ring state: See *Settling with power*

Army Aviation Information Practice Test

1. A helicopter is:

    A. A type of gyrocraft.
    B. A type of rotorcraft.
    C. A category of rotary-wing airplanes.
    D. A sub-group of gyrocopters.

2. Helicopter turbine engines produce _____ thrust per pound than piston engines:

    A. less
    B. the same
    C. more
    D. the same, but only after factoring in the effect of density altitude

3. The main forces acting on a helicopter are:

    A. Induced lift, mass, thrust, and form drag.
    B. Lift, weight, thrust, and drag.
    C. Lift, gravity, air resistance, and rotor vortex drag.
    D. None of the above.

4. Helicopters typically have between __ and __ main rotor blade(s):

    A. 2, 6.
    B. 2, 10.
    C. 3, 8.
    D. 3, 7.

5. Depending on the type of helicopter, main rotor system components can include:

    A. A stabilizer bar, upper and lower swashplates, and counterweights.
    B. Pitch horns, teeter or coning hinges, and blade grips.
    C. Pitch and scissor links, and control rods.
    D. All of the above.

6. The function of the flybar is:

    A. To decrease crosswind thrust on the blades and enhance flight stability by keeping the bar stable as the rotor spins.
    B. To increase crosswind thrust and modify flight stability by allowing the bar to spin at a slower speed than the main rotor.
    C. To decrease crosswind thrust and augment flight stability by maintaining the bar at an acute angle to the main rotor.
    D. To spin in a direction opposite to the main rotor's, thereby reducing induced drag

7. Many helicopters have a horizontal stabilizer located:

   A. On the mast.
   B. On the tail boom.
   C. On the fin.
   D. None of the above.

8. The purpose of the tail rotor is:

   A. To create kinetic energy that is transformed into potential energy as the helicopter climbs.
   B. To produce rotational momentum that is used by the transmission to drive a generator.
   C. To produce an anti-torque force acting perpendicular to the helicopter's longitudinal axis.
   D. All of the above.

9. Wheels on _____ types of helicopters are _____ :

   A. all, retractable (to reduce drag).
   B. some, supplementary to skids.
      C. some, retractable.
   D. all, supplementary to skids.

10. A pilot controls a helicopter using:

    A. Flight instruments, hydraulic actuators, and a cyclic with a twist throttle.
    B. Flight instruments, pedals, two or more throttle levers, and avionics.
    C. Pedals, a throttle with a twist grip, collective link rods, and a cyclic.
    D. Pedals, and a collective, throttle, and cyclic.

11. From a physics perspective, the _____ force is deemed to act through a helicopter's _____ :

    A. lift, center of motion.
    B. total weight, center of gravity.
    C. induced drag, longitudinal axis.
    D. total mass, center of motion.

12. When a pilot banks a helicopter, causing it to turn, _____ :

    A. The machine's weight increases.
    B. The machine's weight remains the same.
    C. The machine's gravitational drag increases.
    D. The vertical component of the lift vector remains the same.

13. In the case of helicopters, lift is produced by _____ moving through the air at a speed sufficient to create _____:

 A. rotor blades, gyroscopic precession.
 B. the flybar, an anti-drag force.
 C. airfoils, a pressure differential.
 D. None of the above.

14. Thrust acts _____ to the aircraft's _____:

 A. at an acute angle, driven portion of the tail rotor disk.
 B. perpendicular, rotational relative wind.
 C. laterally, outer two-thirds of the main rotor disk.
 D. parallel, longitudinal axis.

15. Profile drag consists of _____ created by _____ and _____:

 A. induced drag, angular momentum, aircraft components that do not contribute to lift.
 B. skin friction, surface imperfections, form drag.
 C. an inclined main rotor disk, increasing angle of attack, high blade rpm.
 D. None of the above.

16. Vortices produced by spinning rotor blades create:

 A. Form drag.
 B. Rotational drag.
 C. Parasite drag.
 D. Induced drag.

17. When plotted on a graph, L/DMAX is the point where the helicopter's _____:

 A. Total lift-to-drag ratio is the greatest.
 B. Induced lift-to-drag ratio is maximized.
 C. Perpendicular lift component exceeds the rotational drag vector by at least 50 percent.
 D. Ability to carry pilots, cargo, etc. at the maneuvering speed is most fuel-efficient.

18. A helicopter's potential energy is affected by:

 A. The tail rotor's anti-torque force.
 B. The relative wind.
 C. The aircraft's height above the ground.
 D. All of the above.

19. Which of the following factors affect the lift produced by spinning rotor blades:

    A. Airfoil coefficient of lift.
    B. Air density.
    C. Blade area.
    D. All of the above.

20. What happens when a helicopter's main rotor blades spin rapidly?

    A. The angle of incidence decreases causing more lift on the retreating blades.
    B. The upper and lower sides of each blade experience a difference in pressure.
    C. Gyroscopic precession acts laterally on the aircraft.
    D. The center of pressure on each blade moves forward, creating a vortex.

21. Newton's Third Law of Motion applies to helicopters because:

    A. The spinning main rotor makes the aircraft try to spin in the opposite direction.
    B. Torque is balanced by the longitudinal drag vector.
    C. A ducted-fan helicopter produces less torque than an un-ducted one.
    D. Rotational relative wind opposes the angular momentum force.

22. When the pilot pushes the cyclic forward:

    A. The main rotor disk tilts forward.
    B. The blades' angle of attack on the rearward section of the tail rotor disk decreases.
    C. The angle of attack of the driven portion of the main rotor disk increases.
    D. All of the above.

23. Multi-engine helicopters have:

    A. A supplementary freewheeling clutch.
    B. A coaxial drive shaft and two transmissions.
    C. A throttle lever for each engine.
    D. All of the above.

24. When the pilot wants the helicopter's nose to move left or right, he or she:

    A. Pushes down on the collective for left motion and pulls up on it to turn right.
    B. Tilts the main rotor disk left or right while keeping the pedals neutral.
    C. Pushes on the left or right pedal while adjusting the cyclic to compensate for greater rotational drag.
    D. Pushes on the corresponding pedal.

25. For helicopters with a main rotor disk that spins counter-clockwise, the _____ airflow speed happens when each blade reaches the _____ position:

    A. median, nine o'clock (left)
    B. minimum, three o'clock (right)
    C. maximum, three o'clock (right)
    D. L/DMAX, six o'clock (aft)

26. On the advancing rotor blade, lift _____ and the blade _____:

    A. increases, angles up near the tip due to greater centripetal force.
    B. increases, moves upward.
    C. transitions outward, experiences stronger lateral torque.
    D. None of the above.

27. The angle between the _____ of a rotor blade and its direction of motion relative to the _____ is the angle of attack (AOA), which is _____ angle.:

    A. mean camber line, air, a constant.
    B. chord line, air, an aerodynamic.
    C. chord line, longitudinal airflow, a variable.
    D. mean camber line, longitudinal airflow, an acute.

28. The angle of incidence is between the _____ line of each blade and the rotor system's _____:

    A. mean chamber, forward-flight relative wind.
    B. mean chamber, rotational relative wind.
    C. chord, angular momentum.
    D. chord, plane of rotation.

29. When a helicopter engine _____, a clutch mechanism called a _____:

    A. fails; governing transmission is disconnected from the engine by the pilot, which allows the main rotor to spin freely.
    B. is shutdown after landing; gearbox controller is disconnected from the engine by the pilot, which allows the main and tail rotors to spin freely.
    C. accelerates too rapidly; terminal speed unit automatically disconnects the engine from the tail rotor, allowing it to spin freely.
    D. fails; freewheeling unit automatically disconnects the engine from the main rotor, allowing it to spin freely.

30. During an autorotation in forward flight, the rotor disk takes in _____ air and the driven, driving, and stall regions of each blade move _____ along its length (span), but only on the _____ side of the disk:

    A. upward flowing, outboard, retreating.
    B. downward flowing, inward, advancing.
    C. upward flowing, inward, retreating.
    D. ambient, outward, advancing.

31. Where there is too much lift, the main rotor blades will:

    A. Torque on the retreating blades.
    B. Twist.
    C. Flap.
    D. Create vortices in the driven region.

32. Centrifugal force _____ spinning helicopter main rotor blades _____.

    A. pushes, inward.
    B. pulls, outward.
    C. angles down, during autorotation.
    D. angles up, during liftoff.

33. If left uncorrected, greater lift produced by the advancing side of the rotor disk compared to the lift created by the disk's retreating side could make the helicopter _____:

    A. fly in a sideslip.
    B. vibrate excessively and come apart.
    C. torque clockwise.
    D. uncontrollable.

34. The driven region is _____ the blade tips and normally __ percent of the radius:

    A. nearest, 30.
    B. furthest from, 30.
    C. mid-span from, 50.
    D. nearest, 50.

35. The _____ region is normally between a blade's _____ and _____ regions:

    A. stall, driven, high AOA.
    B. stall, driving, low AOA.
    C. driven, high AOA, stall.
    D. driving, stall, driven.

36. Because of gyroscopic precession, if a wind gust applies a downward force on the left side of a helicopter's main rotor disk as it spins clockwise (as viewed from above), the movement response occurs at the __ o'clock position:

A. 9.
B. 6.
C. 12.
D. 3.

37. Helicopters experience effective translational lift while transitioning to forward flight at approximately __ to __ knots:

A. 20, 28.
B. 10, 20.
C. 16, 24.
D. 12, 24.

38. Maximum ground effect occurs during a hover up to a height equal to ____ percent of the main rotor's diameter:

A. 50.
B. 100.
C. 150.
D. None of the above.

39. A pilot can worsen a helicopter's pendular action by:

A. Applying too much angle of incidence.
B. Over-controlling the aircraft.
C. Moving the cyclic left while pushing on the right pedal.
D. Moving the cyclic left while pulling up on the collective.

40. The phenomenon of a helicopter sinking into its own downwash is called:

A. L/Wmin (minimum lift-to-weight ratio).
B. An airfoil stall.
C. Vortex torque state.
D. Settling with power.

Army Aviation Information Practice Test – Answers

1. B	21. A
2. C	22. A
3. B	23. C
4. A	24. D
5. D	25. C
6. A	26. B
7. B	27. B
8. C	28. D
9. C	29. D
10. D	30. A
11. B	31. C
12. A	32. B
13. C	33. D
14. D	34. A
15. D	35. D
16. D	36. C
17. A	37. C
18. C	38. B
19. D	39. B
20. B	40. D

Chapter 4: Spatial Apperception

The Spatial Apperception section is simple, but deceiving. The best method to beating this section is to use a strategy for each and every question. Missed questions are 99% attributable to the test-taker looking at the question, abandoning their strategy because an answer "just looks right" at first glance. You will have 10 minutes to answer 25 questions, which is actually ample time once you get familiarized with the format.

First, let's review how the test is formatted. On the following page, you'll see there is an image of a horizon, typically with both water and land or some other distinguishable features to use as references. Imagine this is the view from the cockpit of an aircraft. Below this image, you will have 5 multiple choice options. Each option, A through E, shows the aircraft relative to the ground. Your task is to determine which aircraft represents the view from the cockpit.

The absolutely best strategy for this section is to employ a process of elimination and to follow that process strictly for each question. In each answer choice, the aircraft might be diving or climbing or flying level, banking left or right at various degrees or not banking at all, and traveling any direction (inbound, outbound, etc). It is best to start with the easiest and most obvious identifier, banking. For example, if you see that the image from the cockpit is flat and level, you can immediately remove any answer choice with any amount of bank either left or right which is represented by the horizon being tilted at an angle. If the horizon tilts UP to the right, the aircraft is banking right. If the horizon tilts UP to the left, the aircraft is banking left.

Next in the process of elimination, determine if the view from the cockpit is climbing or diving or level. This can be a little trickier because the differences are much more subtle and sometimes hard to distinguish. The best method is to find the vertical center-point of the view from the aircraft. If the horizon is ABOVE the centerpoint, the aircraft is diving. If it is BELOW the centerpoint, the aircraft is climbing. Remember, although it is more subtle than determining whether the aircraft is banking, this section is not intended to be devious such that you will have 5 answer choices of all aircraft in a dive but slightly more or less.

Finally, determine the orientation of the aircraft. For example, if the view from the cockpit shows water from edge to edge, you are obviously flying out to sea. So if there are answer choices showing the aircraft flying inbound to land or flying parallel to the coast, those are obviously incorrect.

This process of elimination can of course be modified for each test-taker. Some people find the orientation of the aircraft the most obvious and easy, so choose to start their process of elimination with that. Often, it is the diving and climbing that unnerves test-takers simply because they over-think it.

Here are some views from the aircraft with the attributable features:

Slight dive, no bank, & flying inbound to land (the "Land" is the dark area, the "water" is indicated with the little lines to represent waves). Notice the horizon is slightly above the center-point.

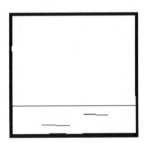

Climbing, no bank, & flying out to sea (note the horizon below the center-point)

Climbing, banking left, flying parallel to land (remember, the horizon slopes UP to the left, so the aircraft is banking left. The horizon is slightly below the center-point, so must be climbing).

Remember that with climbing and diving, the differences can be quite subtle. Do not overthink this! The answer choices are often quite different and by process of elimination, you will likely never encounter any problem where you have 2 or more answer choices that are too similar. Use the process of elimination and the correct answer will reveal itself.

Next, views of the aircraft with attributable features:

- Aircraft flying flat and level, no bank

- Aircraft flying at slight climb, banking left

- Aircraft diving, no bank (possibly slight bank, but depends on viewpoint)

- Aircraft climbing, banking left

Finally, let's look at an example problem and work through it step-by-step:

Remember, you can choose your own order of elimination, just start with whatever attribute is easiest for you to identify. In this case, let's start with direction of travel. In the view from the aircraft, it is obviously flying along the coastline. Therefore, answer choices B and E are immediately out because B is flying out to sea and E is flying inbound to land.

Next, still in terms of direction of travel, the land is on the left side of the image. Because of that, we know answer choice C must be incorrect as the view from the cockpit would have the land on the right side.

We are now down to only choices A and D remaining. As you can see from the view from the aircraft, the horizon is tilted, so we know the aircraft is banking. Without even worrying about what direction it is banking (FYI: it is banking left b/c the horizon slopes UP to the left), we know that answer choice A is incorrect because that aircraft is flat and level.

The only possible answer choice is D. You will note that we did not even get to whether the aircraft was in a climb or dive. In this case, the aircraft in answer choice D appears to be in a very slight climb. This helps illustrate the subtleness of the viewpoint from the cockpit. As you can see, the horizon is slightly below the center-point, although the land does climb slightly higher which can throw some people off. Typically, it's best to look at the water for a reference point since there are no variations in altitude.

Let's get started with the practice test. You will encounter 25 questions on the real test, for which you have 10 minutes to answer. That seems like a short time, but after the first couple of practice questions and get the feel for it, most people notice they can answer the questions easily in under 15-20 seconds. Again, once you get the hang of this section, move on to something else.

Spatial Apperception Practice Test

1.

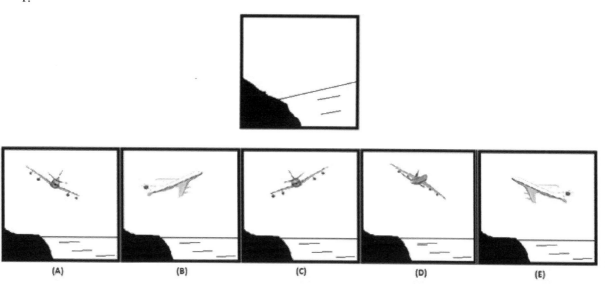

2.

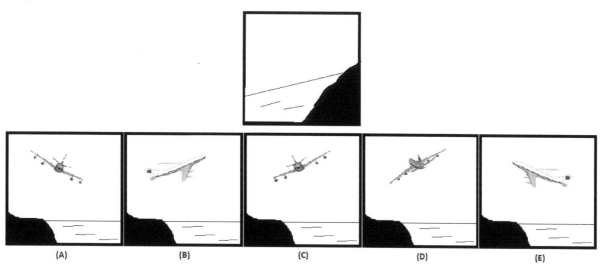

3.

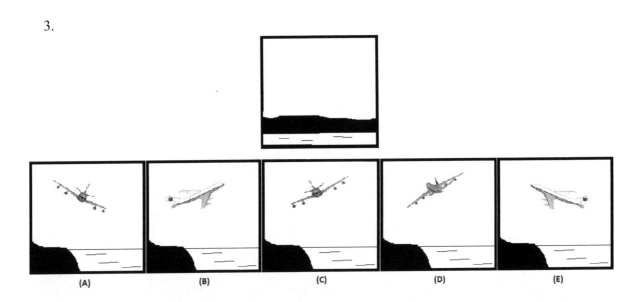

(A)   (B)   (C)   (D)   (E)

4.

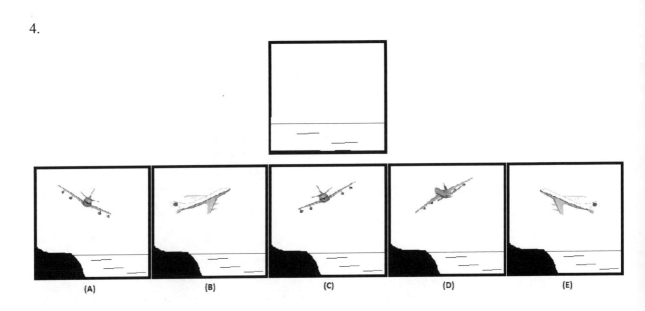

(A)   (B)   (C)   (D)   (E)

5.

(A) (B) (C) (D) (E)

6.

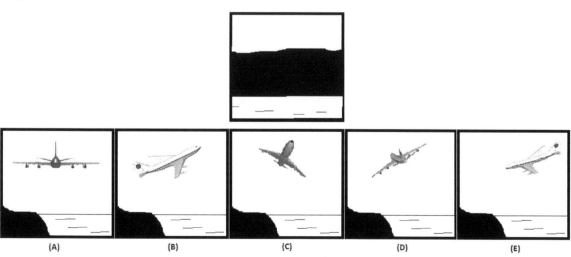

(A) (B) (C) (D) (E)

53

7.

(A)   (B)   (C)   (D)   (E)

8.

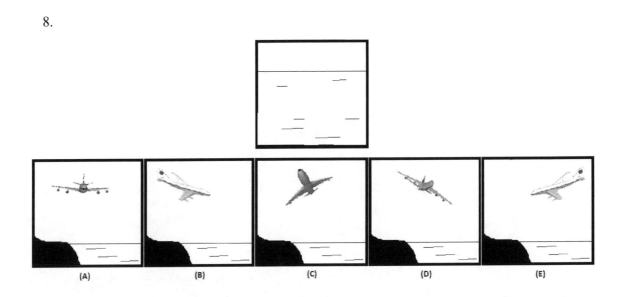

(A)   (B)   (C)   (D)   (E)

9.

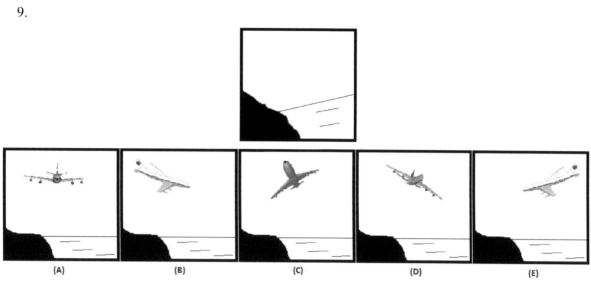

10.

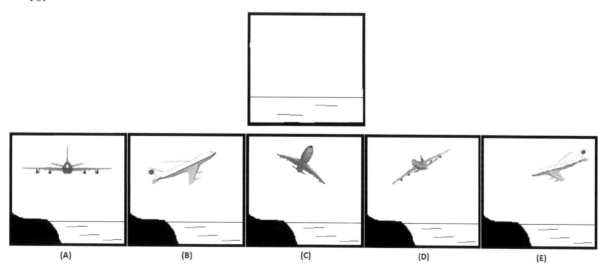

11.

12.

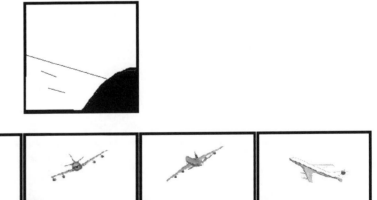

13.

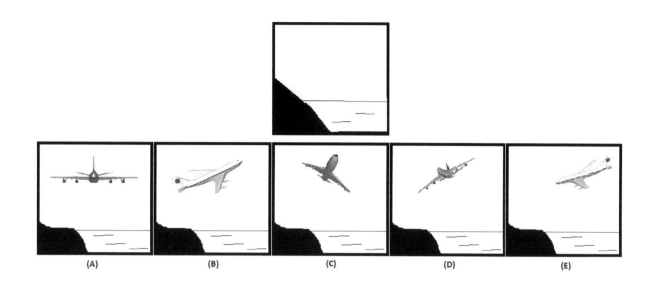

14.

15.

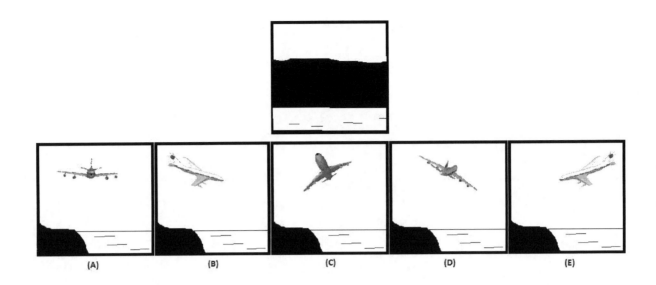

Spatial Apperception Practice Test – Answers

1. D
2. C
3. E
4. B
5. A
6. E
7. C
8. B
9. D
10. B
11. C
12. A
13. A
14. D
15. E

Chapter 5: Reading Comprehension

The Reading Comprehension test measures your ability to understand, analyze, and evaluate written passages. You will be given 20 questions with a 30 minute time limit. The questions will generally be formatted such that you are presented a short passage and asked to find the answer choice that could have been inferred from only the information presented in the passage. The trick of this section is that many of the answer choices might be "true" or "feasible", but you will have to select the "best" answer.

We will cover the methods to best decipher and dissect the necessary information from a passage so that you can more quickly and accurately find the correct answer. After that, there are practice questions to help reinforce the review section so that the Reading Comprehension exam becomes relatively easy for you.

Reading

The Reading section of the exam will assess your ability to summarize, interpret, and draw conclusions about both non-fiction and fiction passages. You'll be asked questions about:

- the main idea of a passage
- the role of supporting details in the passage
- adding supporting details to the passage
- the structure of the passage
- the author's purpose
- logical inferences that can be drawn from the passage
- comparing passages
- understanding vocabulary and figurative language

The SIFT Reading section will require you to read both non-fiction and fiction passages and then answer questions about them. These questions will fall into three main categories:

About the Author: The question will ask about the author's attitude, thoughts, and opinions. When encountering a question asking specifically about the author, pay attention to context clues in the article. The answer may not be explicitly stated but instead conveyed in the overall message.

Passage Facts: You must distinguish between facts and opinions presented in the passage. You may also be asked to identify specific information supplied by the author of the passage.

Additional Information: These questions will have you look at what kind of information could be added to or was missing from the passage. They may also ask in what direction the passage was going. Questions may ask what statement could be added to strengthen the author's statement, or weaken it; they may also provide a fill-in-the-blank option to include a statement that is missing from, but fits with the rest of, the passage.

The Reading section will also include informational source comprehension questions. These questions don't refer back to a text passage; instead, they will ask you to interpret an informational source like a nutrition label, map, or thermometer. (These questions are covered in the section below titled "Informational Source Comprehension.")

Strategies

Despite the different types of questions you will face, there are some strategies for Reading Comprehension which apply across the board:

- Read the answer choices first, then read the passage. This will save you time, as you will know what to look out for as you read.
- Use the process of elimination. Some answer choices are obviously incorrect and are relatively easy to detect. After reading the passage, eliminate those blatantly incorrect answer choices; this increases your chance of finding the correct answer much more quickly.
- Avoid negative statements. Generally, test-makers will not make negative statements about anyone or anything. Statements will be either neutral or positive, so if it seems like an answer choice has a negative connotation, it is very likely that the answer is intentionally false.

The Main Idea

The main idea of a text is the purpose behind why a writer would choose to write a book, article, story, etc. Being able to find and understand the main idea is a critical skill necessary to comprehend and appreciate what you're reading.

Imagine that you're at a friend's home for the evening. He says, "Hey, I think we should watch this movie tonight. Is that ok with you?"

"Yeah, that sounds good," you reply. "What's it about?"

You'd like to know a little about what you'll be watching, but your question may not get you a satisfactory answer, because you've only asked about the topic of the film. The **topic**—what the movie is about—is only half the story. Think, for example, about all the alien invasion films ever been made. While these films may share the same general subject, what they have to say about the aliens or about humanity's theoretical response to invasion may be very different. Each filmmaker has different ideas or opinions she wants to convey about a topic, just as writers write because they have something to say about a particular topic. When you look beyond the facts to the argument the writer is making about his topic, you're looking for the **main idea**.

One more quick note: the exam may also ask about a passage's **theme**, which is similar to but distinct from its topic. While a topic is usually a specific *person, place, thing*, or *issue*, the theme is an *idea* or *concept* that the author refers back to frequently. Examples of common themes include ideas like the importance of family, the dangers of technology, and the beauty of nature.

There will be many questions on the exam that require you to differentiate between the topic, theme, and main idea of a passage. Let's look at an example passage to see how you would answer these questions.

"Babe Didrikson Zaharias, one of the most decorated female athletes of the twentieth century, is an inspiration for everyone. Born in 1911 in Beaumont, Texas, Zaharias lived in a time when women were considered second-class to men, but she never let that stop her from becoming a champion. Babe was one of seven children in a poor immigrant family, and was competitive from an early age. As a child she excelled at most things she tried, especially sports, which continued into high school and beyond. After high school, Babe played amateur basketball for two years, and soon after began training in track and field. Despite the fact that women were only allowed to enter in three events, Babe represented the United States in the 1932 Los Angeles Olympics, and won two gold medals and one silver for track and field events.

"In the early 1930s, Babe began playing golf which earned her a legacy. The first tournament she entered was a men's only tournament, however she did not make the cut to play. Playing golf as an amateur was the only option for a woman at this time, since there was no professional women's league. Babe played as an amateur for a little over a decade, until she turned pro in 1947 for the Ladies Professional Golf Association (LPGA) of which she was a founding member. During her career as a golfer, Babe won eighty-two tournaments, amateur and professional, including the U.S. Women's Open, All-American Open, and British Women's Open Golf Tournament. In 1953, Babe was diagnosed with cancer, but fourteen weeks later, she played in a tournament. That year she won her third U.S. Women's Open. However by 1955, she didn't have the physicality to compete anymore, and she died of the disease in 1956."

The topic of this paragraph is obviously Babe Zaharias—the whole passage describes events from her life. But what is the main idea of this paragraph? You might be tempted to answer, *Babe Zaharias*, or *Babe Zaharias' life*. Yes, Babe Zaharias' life is the topic of the passage—who or what the passage is about—but the topic is not the main idea. The main idea is what the writer wants to say about this subject. What is the writer saying about Babe Zaharias' life? She's saying that she's someone to admire—that's the main idea and what unites all the information in the paragraph. Lastly, what might the theme of the passage be? The writer refers to several broad concepts, including never giving up and overcoming the odds, both of which could be themes for the passage.

The example above shows two important characteristics of a main idea:

- It is general enough to encompass all of the ideas in the passage. The main idea of a passage should be broad enough for all of the other sentences in that passage to fit underneath it, like people under an umbrella.

- It asserts a specific viewpoint that the author supports with facts, opinions, or other details. In other words, the main idea takes a stand.

Example

From so far away it's easy to imagine the surface of our solar system's planets as enigmas—how could we ever know what those far-flung planets really look like? It turns out, however, that scientists have a number of tools at their disposal that allow them to paint detailed pictures of many planets' surfaces. The topography of Venus, for example, has been explored by several space probes, including the Russian Venera landers and NASA's Magellan orbiter. These craft used imaging and radar to map the surface of the planet, identifying a whole host of features including volcanoes, craters, and a complex system of channels. Mars has similarly been mapped by space probes, including the famous Mars Rovers, which are automated vehicles that actually landed on the surface of Mars. These rovers have been used by NASA and other space agencies to study the geology, climate, and possible biology of the planet.

In addition these long-range probes, NASA has also used its series of orbiting telescopes to study distant planets. These four massively powerful telescopes include the famous Hubble Space Telescope as well as the Compton Gamma Ray Observatory, Chandra X-Ray Observatory, and the Spitzer Space Telescope. Scientists can use these telescopes to examine planets using not only visible light but also infrared and near-infrared light, ultraviolet light, x-rays and gamma rays.
Powerful telescopes aren't just found in space: NASA makes use of Earth-bound telescopes as well. Scientists at the National Radio Astronomy Observatory in Charlottesville, VA, have spent decades using radio imaging to build an incredibly detailed portrait of Venus' surface. In fact, Earth-bound telescopes offer a distinct advantage over orbiting telescopes because they allow scientists to capture data from a fixed point, which in turn allows them to effectively compare data collected over long period of time.

Which of the following sentences best describes the main of the passage?
A)   It's impossible to know what the surfaces of other planets are really like.
B)   Telescopes are an important tool for scientists studying planets in our solar system.
C)   Venus' surface has many of the same features as the Earth's, including volcanoes, craters, and channels.
D)   Scientists use a variety of advanced technologies to study the surface of the planets in our solar system.

Answer: Answer A) can be eliminated because it directly contradicts the rest of the passage, which goes into detail about how scientists have learned about the surfaces of other planets. Answers B) and C) can also be eliminated because they offer only specific details from the passage—while both choices contain details from the passage, neither is general enough to encompass the passage as a whole. Only answer D) provides an assertion that is both backed up by the passage's content and general enough to cover the entire passage.

Topic and Summary Sentences

Writers sometimes lead with preliminary sentences that give the reader clear ideas of what the text is about. A sentence that encompasses the main idea of the text is the topic sentence.

Notice, for example, how the first sentence in the example paragraph about Babe Zaharias states the main idea: *Babe Didrikson Zaharias, one of the most decorated female athletes of the twentieth century, is an inspiration for everyone.*

Topic sentences are often found at the beginning of paragraphs. Sometimes, though, writers begin with specific supporting details and lead up to the main idea; in this case the topic sentence is found at the end of the paragraph. In other cases there isn't a clear topic sentence at all—but that doesn't mean there isn't a main idea; the author has just chosen not to express it in a clear topic sentence. You may also see a **summary sentence** at the end of a passage. As its name suggests, this sentence sums up the passage, often by restating the main idea and the author's key evidence supporting it.

Example

In the following paragraph, what are the topic and summary sentences?

The Constitution of the United States establishes a series of limits to rein in centralized power. Separation of powers distributes federal authority among three competing branches: the executive, the legislative, and the judicial. Checks and balances allow the branches to check the usurpation of power by any one branch. States' rights are protected under the Constitution from too much encroachment by the federal government. Enumeration of powers names the specific and few powers the federal government has. These four restrictions have helped sustain the American republic for over two centuries.

Answer: The topic sentence is the first sentence in the paragraph. It introduces the topic of discussion, in this case the constitutional limits aimed at resisting centralized power. The summary sentence is the last sentence in the paragraph. It sums up the information that was just presented: here, that constitutional limits have helped sustain the United States of America for over two hundred years.

Implied Main Idea

When there's no clear topic sentence, you're looking for an **implied main idea**. This requires some detective work: you will need to look at the author's word choice and tone in addition to the content of the passage to find his or her main idea. Let's look at an example paragraph.

"One of my summer reading books was *Mockingjay*. Though it's several hundred pages long, I read it in just a few days. I couldn't wait to see what happened to Katniss, the main character. But by the time I got to the end, I wondered if I should have spent my week doing something else. The ending was such a letdown that I completely forgot that I'd enjoyed most of the book."

There's no topic sentence here, but you should still be able to find the main idea. Look carefully at what the writer says and how she says it. What is she suggesting?
A)   *Mockingjay* is a terrific novel.
B)   *Mockingjay* is disappointing.
C)   *Mockingjay* is full of suspense.
D)   *Mockingjay* is a lousy novel.

Answer: The correct answer is B): the novel is disappointing. How can you tell that this is the main idea? First, you can eliminate choice C) because it's too specific to be a main idea. It only deals with one specific aspect of the novel (its suspense).

Sentences A), B), and D), on the other hand, all express a larger idea about the quality of the novel. However, only one of these statements can actually serve as a "net" for the whole paragraph. Notice that while the first few sentences praise the novel, the last two criticize it. Clearly, this is a mixed review.

Therefore, the best answer is B). Sentence A) is too positive and doesn't account for the "letdown" of an ending. Sentence D), on the other hand, is too negative and doesn't account for the reader's sense of suspense and interest in the main character. But sentence B) allows for both positive and negative aspects—when a good thing turns bad, we often feel disappointed.

Example
Fortunately, none of Alyssa's coworkers has ever seen inside the large filing drawer in her desk. Disguised by the meticulous neatness of the rest of her workspace, there was no sign of the chaos beneath. To even open it, she had to struggle for several minutes with the enormous pile of junk jamming the drawer, until it would suddenly give way, and papers, folders, and candy wrappers spilled out of the top and onto the floor. It was an organizational nightmare, with torn notes and spreadsheets haphazardly thrown on top of each other, and melted candy smeared across pages. She was worried the odor would soon permeate to her coworker's desks, revealing to them her secret.

Which of the following expresses the main idea of this paragraph?
A)   Alyssa wishes she could move to a new desk.
B)   Alyssa wishes she had her own office.
C)   Alyssa is glad none of her coworkers know about her messy drawer.
D)   Alyssa is sad because she doesn't have any coworkers.

Answer: What the paragraph adds up to is that Alyssa is terribly embarrassed about her messy drawer, and she's glad that none of her coworkers have seen it, making C) the correct answer choice. This is the main idea. The paragraph opens with the word "fortunately," so we know that she thinks it's a good thing that none of her coworkers have seen inside the drawer. Plus, notice how the drawer is described: "it was an organizational nightmare," and it apparently doesn't even function properly – "to even open the drawer, she had to struggle for several minutes…" The writer reveals that it has an odor, with "melted candy" inside. Alyssa is clearly ashamed of her drawer and worries about what her coworkers would think if they saw inside it.

Supporting Details

Supporting details provide more support for the author's main idea. For instance, in the Babe Zaharias example above, the writer makes the general assertion that *Babe Didrikson Zaharias, one of the most decorated female athletes of the twentieth century, is an inspiration for everyone*. The other sentences offer specific facts and details that prove why Babe Zaharias is an inspiration: the struggles she faced as a female athlete, and the specific years she competed in the Olympics and in golf.

Writers often provide clues that can help you identify supporting details. These **signal words** tell you that a supporting fact or idea will follow, and so can be helpful in identifying supporting details. Signal words can also help you rule out sentences that are not the main idea or topic sentence: if a sentence begins with one of these phrases, it will likely be too specific to be a main idea.

Questions on the SIFT will ask you to do two things with supporting details: you will need to find details that support a particular idea and also explain why a particular detail was included in the passage. In order to answer these questions, you need to have a solid understanding of the passage's main idea. With this knowledge, you can determine how a supporting detail fits in with the larger structure of the passage.

Example
From so far away it's easy to imagine the surface of our solar system's planets as enigmas—how could we ever know what those far-flung planets really look like? It turns out, however, that scientists have a number of tools at their disposal that allow them to paint detailed pictures of many planets' surfaces. The topography of Venus, for example, has been explored by several space probes, including the Russian *Venera* landers and NASA's *Magellan* orbiter. These craft used imaging and radar to map the surface of the planet, identifying a whole host of features including volcanoes, craters, and a complex system of channels. Mars has similarly been mapped by space probes, including the famous Mars Rovers, which are automated vehicles that actually landed on the surface of Mars. These rovers have been used by NASA and other space agencies to study the geology, climate, and possible biology of the planet.

In addition these long-range probes, NASA has also used its series of orbiting telescopes to study distant planets. These four massively powerful telescopes include the famous Hubble Space Telescope as well as the Compton Gamma Ray Observatory, Chandra X-Ray Observatory, and the Spitzer Space Telescope. Scientists can use these telescopes to examine planets using not only visible light but also infrared and near-infrared light, ultraviolet light, x-rays and gamma rays.
Powerful telescopes aren't just found in space: NASA makes use of Earth-bound telescopes as well. Scientists at the National Radio Astronomy Observatory in

Charlottesville, VA, have spent decades using radio imaging to build an incredibly detailed portrait of Venus' surface. In fact, Earth-bound telescopes offer a distinct advantage over orbiting telescopes because they allow scientists to capture data from a fixed point, which in turn allows them to effectively compare data collected over long period of time.

Which sentence from the text best helps develop the idea that scientists make use of many different technologies to study the surfaces of other planets?

A)   These rovers have been used by NASA and other space agencies to study the geology, climate, and possible biology of the planet.

B)   From so far away it's easy to imagine the surface of our solar system's planets as enigmas—how could we ever know what those far-flung planets really look like?

C)   In addition these long-range probes, NASA has also used its series of orbiting telescopes to study distant planets.

D)   These craft used imaging and radar to map the surface of the planet, identifying a whole host of features including volcanoes, craters, and a complex system of channels.

Answer: You're looking for detail from the passage that supports the main idea—scientists make use of many different technologies to study the surfaces of other planets. Answer A) includes a specific detail about rovers, but does not offer any details that support the idea of multiple technologies being used. Similarly, answer D) provides another specific detail about space probes. Answer B) doesn't provide any supporting details; it simply introduces the topic of the passage. Only answer C) provides a detail that directly supports the author's assertion that scientists use multiple technologies to study the planets.

If true, which detail could be added to the passage above to support the author's argument that scientists use many different technologies to study the surface of planets?

A)   Because the Earth's atmosphere blocks x-rays, gamma rays, and infrared radiation, NASA needed to put telescopes in orbit above the atmosphere.

B)   In 2015, NASA released a map of Venus which was created by compiling images from orbiting telescopes and long-range space probes.

C)   NASA is currently using the *Curiosity* and *Opportunity* rovers to look for signs of ancient life on Mars.

D)   NASA has spent over $2.5 billion to build, launch, and repair the Hubble Space Telescope.

Answer: You can eliminate answers C) and D) because they don't address the topic of studying the surface of planets. Answer A) can also be eliminated because it only addresses a single technology. Only choice B) provides would add support to the author's claim about the importance of using multiple technologies.

The author likely included the detail *Earth-bound telescopes offer a distinct advantage over orbiting telescopes because they allow scientists to capture data from a fixed point* in order to:

A)   Explain why it has taken scientists so long to map the surface of Venus.

B)   Suggest that Earth-bound telescopes are the most important equipment used by NASA scientists.

C)   Prove that orbiting telescopes will soon be replaced by Earth-bound telescopes.

D)   Demonstrate why NASA scientists rely on my different types of scientific equipment.

Answer: Only answer D) directs directly to the author's main argument. The author doesn't mention how long it has taken to map the surface of Venus (answer A), nor does he say that one technology is more important than the others (answer B). And while this detail does highlight the advantages of using Earth-bound telescopes, the author's argument is that many technologies are being used at the same time, so there's no reason to think that orbiting telescopes will be replaced (answer C).

Text Structure

Authors can structure passages in a number of different ways. These distinct organizational patterns, referred to as **text structure**, use the logical relationships between ideas to improve the readability and coherence of a text. The most common ways passages are organized include:

- **problem-solution**: the author presents a problem and then discusses a solution
- **comparison-contrast**: the author presents two situations and then discusses the similarities and differences
- **cause-effect**: the author presents an action and then discusses the resulting effects
- **descriptive**: an idea, object, person, or other item is described in detail

Example

The issue of public transportation has begun to haunt the fast-growing cities of the southern United States. Unlike their northern counterparts, cities like Atlanta, Dallas, and Houston have long promoted growth out and not up—these are cities full of sprawling suburbs and single-family homes, not densely concentrated skyscrapers and apartments. What to do then, when all those suburbanites need to get into the central business districts for work? For a long time it seemed highways were the answer: twenty-lane wide expanses of concrete that would allow commuters to move from home to work and back again. But these modern miracles have become time-sucking, pollution spewing nightmares. They may not like it, but it's time for these cities to turn toward public transport like trains and buses if they want their cities to remain livable.

The organization of this passage can best be described as:

A)   a comparison of two similar ideas
B)   a description of a place
C)   a discussion of several effects all related to the same cause
D)   a discussion of a problem followed by the suggestion of a solution

Answer: You can exclude answer choice C) because the author provides no root cause or a list of effects. From there this question gets tricky, because the passage contains structures similar to those described above. For example, it compares two things (cities in the North and South) and describes a place (a sprawling city). However, if you look at the overall organization of the passage, you can see that it starts by presenting a problem (transportation) and then presents a solution (trains and buses), making answer D) the only choice that encompasses the entire passage.

The Author's Purpose
Whenever an author writes a text, she always has a purpose, whether that's to entertain, inform, explain, or persuade. A short story, for example, is meant to entertain, while an online news article would be designed to inform the public about a current event.
Each of these different types of writing has a specific name. On the exam, you will be asked to identify which of these categories a passage fits into:

- **Narrative writing** tells a story. (novel, short story, play)
- **Expository writing** informs people. (newspaper and magazine articles)
- **Technical writing** explains something. (product manual, directions)
- **Persuasive writing** tries to convince the reader of something. (opinion column on a blog)

You may also be asked about primary and secondary sources. These terms describe not the writing itself but the author's relationship to what's being written about. A **primary source** is an unaltered piece of writing that was composed during the time when the events being described took place; these texts are often written by the people involved. A **secondary source** might address the same topic but provides extra commentary or analysis. These texts can be written by people not directly involved in the events. For example, a book written by a political candidate to inform people about his or her stand on an issue is a primary source; an online article written by a journalist analyzing how that position will affect the election is a secondary source.

Example
Elizabeth closed her eyes and braced herself on the armrests that divided her from her fellow passengers. Take-off was always the worst part for her. The revving of the engines, the way her stomach dropped as the plane lurched upward: it made her feel sick. Then, she had to watch the world fade away beneath her, getting smaller and smaller until it was just her and the clouds hurtling through the sky. Sometimes (but only sometimes) it just had to be endured, though. She focused on the thought of her sister's smiling face and her new baby nephew as the plane slowly pulled onto the runway.

The passage above is reflective of which type of writing?
A) Narrative
B) Expository
C) Technical
D) Persuasive

Answer: The passage is telling a story—we meet Elizabeth and learn about her fear of flying—so it's a narrative text. There is no factual information presented or explained, nor is the author trying to persuade the reader.

Facts vs. Opinions

On the exam Reading passages you might be asked to identify a statement in a passage as either a fact or an opinion, so you'll need to know the difference between the two. A **fact** is a statement or thought that can be proven to be true. The statement *Wednesday comes after Tuesday* is a fact—you can point to a calendar to prove it. In contrast, an **opinion** is an assumption that is not based in fact and cannot be proven to be true. The assertion that *television is more entertaining than feature films* is an opinion—people will disagree on this, and there's no reference you can use to prove or disprove it.

Example
Exercise is critical for healthy development in children. Today, there is an epidemic of unhealthy children in the United States who will face health problems in adulthood due to poor diet and lack of exercise as children. This is a problem for all Americans, especially with the rising cost of healthcare.
It is vital that school systems and parents encourage their children to engage in a minimum of thirty minutes of cardiovascular exercise each day, mildly increasing their heart rate for a sustained period. This is proven to decrease the likelihood of developmental diabetes, obesity, and a multitude of other health problems. Also, children need a proper diet rich in fruits and vegetables so that they can grow and develop physically, as well as learn healthy eating habits early on.

Which of the following is a fact in the passage, not an opinion?
A) Fruits and vegetables are the best way to help children be healthy.
B) Children today are lazier than they were in previous generations.
C) The risk of diabetes in children is reduced by physical activity.
D) Children should engage in thirty minutes of exercise a day.

Answer: Choice B) can be discarded immediately because it is negative and is not discussed anywhere in the passage. Answers A) and D) are both opinions—the author is promoting exercise, fruits, and vegetables as a way to make children healthy. (Notice that these incorrect answers contain words that hint at being an opinion such as *best*, *should*, or other comparisons.) Answer B), on the other hand, is a simple fact stated by the author; it's introduced by the word *proven* to indicate that you don't need to just take the author's word for it.

Drawing Conclusions

In addition to understanding the main idea and factual content of a passage, you'll also be asked to take your analysis one step further and anticipate what other information could logically be added to the passage. In a non-fiction passage, for example, you might be asked which statement the author of the passage would agree with. In an excerpt from a fictional work, you might be asked to anticipate what the character would do next.

To answer these questions, you need to have a solid understanding of the topic, theme, and main idea of the passage; armed with this information, you can figure out which of the answer choices best fits within those criteria (or alternatively, which ones do not). For example, if the author of the passage is advocating for safer working conditions in textile factories, any supporting details that would be added to the passage should support that idea. You might add sentences that contain information about the number of accidents that occur in textile factories or that outline a new plan for fire safety.

Example

Today, there is an epidemic of unhealthy children in the United States who will face health problems in adulthood due to poor diet and lack of exercise during their childhood. This is a problem for all Americans, as adults with chronic health issues are adding to the rising cost of healthcare. A child who grows up living an unhealthy lifestyle is likely to become an adult who does the same.

Because exercise is critical for healthy development in children, it is vital that school systems and parents encourage their children to engage in a minimum of thirty minutes of cardiovascular exercise each day. Even this small amount of exercise has been proven to decrease the likelihood that young people will develop diabetes, obesity, and other health issues as adults. In addition to exercise, children need a proper diet rich in fruits and vegetables so that they can grow and develop physically. Starting a good diet early also teaches children healthy eating habits they will carry into adulthood.

The author of this passage would most likely agree with which statement?
A)   Parents are solely responsible for the health of their children.
B)   Children who do not want to exercise should not be made to.
C)   Improved childhood nutrition will help lower the amount Americans spend on healthcare.
D)   It's not important to teach children healthy eating habits because they will learn them as adults.

Answer: The author would most likely support answer C): he mentions in the first paragraph that unhealthy habits are adding to the rising cost of healthcare. The main idea of the passage is that nutrition and exercise are important for children, so answer B) doesn't make sense—the author would likely support measures to encourage children to exercise. Answers A) and D) can also be eliminated because they are directly contradicted in the text. The author specifically mentions the role of schools systems, so he doesn't believe parents are solely responsible for their children's health. He also specifically states that children who grow up with unhealthy habit will become adults with unhealthy habits, which contradicts D).

Elizabeth closed her eyes and braced herself on the armrests that divided her from her fellow passengers. Take-off was always the worst part for her. The revving of the engines, the way her stomach dropped as the plane lurched upward: it made her feel sick. Then, she had to watch the world fade away beneath her, getting smaller and smaller until it was just her and the clouds hurtling through the sky. Sometimes (but only sometimes) it just had to be endured, though. She focused on the thought of her sister's smiling face and her new baby nephew as the plane slowly pulled onto the runway.

Which of the following is Elizabeth least likely to do in the future?
A)   Take a flight to her brother's wedding.
B)   Apply for a job as a flight attendant.
C)   Never board an airplane again.
D)   Get sick on an airplane.

Answer: It's clear from the passage that Elizabeth hates flying, but it willing to endure it for the sake of visiting her family. Thus, it seems likely that she would be willing to get on a plane for her brother's wedding, making A) and C) incorrect answers. The passage also explicitly tells us that she feels sick on planes, so D) is likely to happen. We can infer, though, that she would not enjoy being on an airplane for work, so she's very unlikely to apply for a job as a flight attendant, which is choice B).

Meaning of Words and Phrases

On the Reading section you may also be asked to provide definitions or intended meanings for words within passages. You may have never encountered some of these words before the test, but there are tricks you can use to figure out what they mean.

Context Clues
The most fundamental vocabulary skill is using the context in which a word is used to determine its meaning. Your ability to observe sentences closely is extremely useful when it comes to understanding new vocabulary words.
There are two types of context that can help you understand the meaning of unfamiliar words: situational context and sentence context. Regardless of which context is present, these types of questions are not really testing your knowledge of vocabulary; rather, they test your ability to comprehend the meaning of a word through its usage.

Situational context is context that is presented by the setting or circumstances in which a word or phrase occurs. **Sentence context** occurs within the specific sentence that contains the vocabulary word. To figure out words using sentence context clues, you should first determine the most important words in the sentence.

There are four types of clues that can help you understand context, and therefore the meaning of a word:

- **Restatement** clues occur when the definition of the word is clearly stated in the sentence.
- **Positive/negative clues** can tell you whether a word has a positive or negative meaning.
- **Contrast clues** include the opposite meaning of a word. Words like *but, on the other hand,* and *however* are tip-offs that a sentence contains a contrast clue.
- **Specific detail clues** provide a precise detail that can help you understand the meaning of the word.

It is important to remember that more than one of these clues can be present in the same sentence. The more there are, the easier it will be to determine the meaning of the word. For example, the following sentence uses both restatement and positive/negative clues: *Janet suddenly found herself destitute, so poor she could barely afford to eat.* The second part of the sentence clearly indicates that *destitute* is a negative word. It also restates the meaning: very poor.

Examples

I had a hard time reading her *illegible* handwriting.
A)   neat
B)   unsafe
C)   sloppy
D)   educated

Answer: Already, you know that this sentence is discussing something that is hard to read. Look at the word that *illegible* is describing: handwriting. Based on context clues, you can tell that *illegible* means that her handwriting is hard to read.

Next, look at the answer choices. Choice A), *neat,* is obviously a wrong answer because neat handwriting would not be difficult to read. Choices B) and D), *unsafe* and *educated,* don't make sense. Therefore, choice C), *sloppy,* is the best answer.

The dog was *dauntless* in the face of danger, braving the fire to save the girl trapped inside the building.
A)   difficult
B)   fearless
C)   imaginative
D)   startled

Answer: Demonstrating bravery in the face of danger would be B) *fearless.* In this case, the restatement clue (*braving the fire*) tells you exactly what the word means.

Beth did not spend any time preparing for the test, but Tyrone kept a *rigorous* study schedule.
A)   strict
B)   loose
C)   boring
D)   strange

Answer: In this case, the contrast word *but* tells us that Tyrone studied in a different way than Beth, which means it's a contrast clue. If Beth did not study hard, then Tyrone did. The best answer, therefore, is choice A).

Analyzing Words

As you no doubt know, determining the meaning of a word can be more complicated than just looking in a dictionary. A word might have more than one **denotation**, or definition; which one the author intends can only be judged by looking at the surrounding text. For example, the word *quack* can refer to the sound a duck makes, or to a person who publicly pretends to have a qualification which he or she does not actually possess.

A word may also have different **connotations**, which are the implied meanings and emotion a word evokes in the reader. For example, a cubicle is a simply a walled desk in an office, but for many the word implies a constrictive, uninspiring workplace. Connotations can vary greatly between cultures and even between individuals.

Lastly, authors might make use of **figurative language**, which is the use of a word to imply something other than the word's literal definition. This is often done by comparing two things. If you say *I felt like a butterfly when I got a new haircut*, the listener knows you don't resemble an insect but instead felt beautiful and transformed.

Word Structure

Although you are not expected to know every word in the English language for your test, you will need the ability to use deductive reasoning to find the choice that is the best match for the word in question, which is why we are going to explain how to break a word into its parts to determine its meaning. Many words can be broken down into three main parts:

prefix – root – suffix

Roots are the building blocks of all words. Every word is either a root itself or has a root. Just as a plant cannot grow without roots, neither can vocabulary, because a word must have a root to give it meaning. The root is what is left when you strip away all the prefixes and suffixes from a word. For example, in the word *unclear*, if you take away the prefix *un-*, you have the root *clear*.

Roots are not always recognizable words, because they generally come from Latin or Greek words, such as *nat*, a Latin root meaning born. The word *native*, which means a person born in a referenced placed, comes from this root, so does the word *prenatal*, meaning before birth. It's important to keep in mind, however, that roots do not always match the exact definitions of words, and they can have several different spellings. **Prefixes** are syllables added to the beginning of a word and **suffixes** are syllables added to the end of the word. Both carry assigned meanings and can be attached to a word to completely change the word's meaning or to enhance the word's original meaning.

Let's use the word prefix itself as an example: *fix* means to place something securely and *pre-* means before. Therefore, *prefix* means to place something before or in front. Now let's look at a suffix: in the word *feminism, femin* is a root which means female. The suffix *-ism* means act, practice, or process. Thus, *feminism* is the process of establishing equal rights for women.

Although you cannot determine the meaning of a word by a prefix or suffix alone, you can use this knowledge to eliminate answer choices; understanding whether the word is positive or negative can give you the partial meaning of the word.

Reading Comprehension Practice Test

This passage is taken from "Peter Pan" by J.M. Barrie:

I don't know whether you have ever seen a map of a person's mind. Doctors sometimes draw maps of other parts of you, and your own map can become intensely interesting, but catch them trying to draw a map of a child's mind, which is not only confused, but keeps going round all the time. There are zigzag lines on it, just like your temperature on a card, and these are probably roads in the island, for the Neverland is always more or less an island, with astonishing splashes of color here and there, and coral reefs and rakish-looking craft in the offing, and savages and lonely lairs, and gnomes who are mostly tailors, and caves through which a river runs, and princes with six elder brothers, and a hut fast going to decay, and one very small old lady with a hooked nose. It would be an easy map if that were all, but there is also first day at school, religion, fathers, the round pond, needle-work, murders, hangings, verbs that take the dative, chocolate pudding day, getting into braces, say ninety-nine, three-pence for pulling out your tooth yourself, and so on, and either these are part of the island or they are another map showing through, and it is all rather confusing, especially as nothing will stand still.

1. What is the main idea of the passage?
   a. Children's minds are simpler than adult minds.
   b. Children's minds are more complex than adult minds.
   c. No one can map the human mind.
   d. Doctors can map children's minds.

2. Which statement is not a detail from the passage?
   a. Peter Pan lives in Neverland.
   b. Neverland is more or less an island.
   c. Gnomes are mostly tailors.
   d. There is chocolate pudding day.

3. What is the meaning of <u>rakish</u> in the middle of the paragraph?
   a. Zigzag
   b. Sailing
   c. Sinking
   d. Streamlined

4. What is the author's primary purpose in writing this passage?
   a. To entertain young readers
   b. To entertain adult readers
   c. To educate children about Neverland
   d. To explain the existence of Neverland

5. Which is the best summary of this passage?
    a. Children's minds are jumbled and confusing.
    b. Adult minds are jumbled and confusing.
    c. Children think about mundane things.
    d. Children are imaginative.

This passage is taken from "Sense and Sensibility" by Jane Austen:

The situation of the house was good. High hills rose immediately behind, and at no great distance on each side; some of which were open downs, the others cultivated and woody. The village of Barton was chiefly on one of these hills, and formed a pleasant view from the cottage windows. The prospect in front was more extensive; it commanded the whole of the valley, and reached into the country beyond. The hills which surrounded the cottage terminated the valley in that direction; under another name, and in another course, it branched out again between two of the steepest of them.

With the size and furniture of the house Mrs. Dashwood was upon the whole well satisfied; for though her former style of life rendered many additions to the latter indispensable, yet to add and improve was a delight to her; and she had at this time ready money enough to supply all that was wanted of greater elegance to the apartments. "As for the house itself, to be sure," said she, "it is too small for our family, but we will make ourselves tolerably comfortable for the present, as it is too late in the year for improvements. Perhaps in the spring, if I have plenty of money, as I dare say I shall, we may think about building. These parlors are both too small for such parties of our friends as I hope to see often collected here; and I have some thoughts of throwing the passage into one of them with perhaps a part of the other, and so leave the remainder of that other for an entrance; this, with a new drawing room which may be easily added, and a bed-chamber and garret above, will make it a very snug little cottage. I could wish the stairs were handsome. But one must not expect everything; though, I suppose it would be no difficult matter to widen them. I shall see how much I am before-hand with the world in the spring, and we will plan our improvements accordingly."

6. What is the main idea of the passage?
    a. The house is well-placed.
    b. The house is too small.
    c. The house could be improved.
    d. The house is quite poor.

7. Which statement is not a detail from the passage?
    a. The parlors are too small.
    b. There is a garret above the drawing room.
    c. The cottage has hills behind it.
    d. Mrs. Dashwood has nice furnishings.

8. What is the meaning of <u>indispensable</u> in the second paragraph?
   a. Necessary
   b. Unnecessary
   c. Unappealing
   d. Appealing

9. What is the author's primary purpose in writing this passage?
   a. To create a visual impression of the house
   b. To provide insights into Mrs. Dashwood's character
   c. To show how Mrs. Dashwood felt about the cottage
   d. To illustrate Mrs. Dashwood's financial state

10. Which is the best summary of this passage?
   a. Mrs. Dashwood finds the cottage lovely, but inadequate.
   b. Mrs. Dashwood would like a smaller home.
   c. Mrs. Dashwood is quite wealthy.
   d. Mrs. Dashwood is impoverished.

This passage is taken from "Myths and Legends of Ancient Greece and Rome" by E. M. Berens:

The division of the world being now satisfactorily arranged, it would seem that all things ought to have gone on smoothly, but such was not the case. Trouble arose in an unlooked-for quarter. The Giants, those hideous monsters (some with legs formed of serpents) who had sprung from the earth and the blood of Uranus, declared war against the triumphant deities of Olympus, and a struggle ensued, which, in consequence of Gæa having made these children of hers invincible as long as they kept their feet on the ground, was wearisome and protracted. Their mother's precaution, however, was rendered unavailing by pieces of rock being hurled upon them, which threw them down, and their feet being no longer placed firmly on their mother-earth, they were overcome, and this tedious war (which was called the Gigantomachia) at last came to an end. Among the most daring of these earth-born giants were Enceladus, Rhœtus, and the valiant Mimas, who, with youthful fire and energy, hurled against heaven great masses of rock and burning oak-trees, and defied the lightning of Zeus. One of the most powerful monsters who opposed Zeus in this war was called Typhon or Typhœus. He was the youngest son of Tartarus and Gæa, and had a hundred heads, with eyes which struck terror to the beholders, and awe-inspiring voices frightful to hear. This dreadful monster resolved to conquer both gods and men, but his plans were at length defeated by Zeus, who, after a violent encounter, succeeded in destroying him with a thunderbolt, but not before he had so terrified the gods that they had fled for refuge to Egypt, where they metamorphosed themselves into different animals and thus escaped.

11. What is the main idea of the passage?
   a. Zeus had to fight the Giants
   b. Gæa was the mother of the gods.
   c. Gæa was the mother of the Giants.

d. The Giants won the battle.
12. Which statement is not a detail from the passage?
   a. Zeus was called Typhon
   b. Zeus was the son of Gaea
   c. Zeus was the husband of Hera
   d. Zeus was the son of Tartarus

13. What is the meaning of <u>triumphant</u> in the paragraph?
   a. Failing
   b. Greek
   c. Victorious
   d. Immoral

14. What is the author's primary purpose in writing this passage?
   a. To entertain the reader
   b. To share stories from mythology
   c. To provide religious education
   d. To show why Greek mythology is wrong

15. Which is the best summary of this passage?
   a. The Giants were monstrous and evil.
   b. The Greek gods of Olympus had to defeat the Giants.
   c. The Giants are the precursors of the gods.
   d. Greek mythology is violent.

This passage is taken from "Anne of Green Gables" by L.M. Montgomery:

"Oh, I can carry it," the child responded cheerfully. "It isn't heavy. I've got all my worldly goods in it, but it isn't heavy. And if it isn't carried in just a certain way the handle pulls out—so I'd better keep it because I know the exact knack of it. It's an extremely old carpet-bag. Oh, I'm very glad you've come, even if it would have been nice to sleep in a wild cherry-tree. We've got to drive a long piece, haven't we? Mrs. Spencer said it was eight miles. I'm glad because I love driving. Oh, it seems so wonderful that I'm going to live with you and belong to you. I've never belonged to anybody—not really. But the asylum was the worst. I've only been in it four months, but that was enough. I don't suppose you ever were an orphan in an asylum, so you can't possibly understand what it is like. It's worse than anything you could imagine. Mrs. Spencer said it was wicked of me to talk like that, but I didn't mean to be wicked. It's so easy to be wicked without knowing it, isn't it? They were good, you know—the asylum people. But there is so little scope for the imagination in an asylum—only just in the other orphans. It was pretty interesting to imagine things about them—to imagine that perhaps the girl who sat next to you was really the daughter of a belted earl, who had been stolen away from her parents in her infancy by a cruel nurse who died before she could confess. I used to lie awake at nights and imagine things like that, because I didn't have time in the day. I guess that's why I'm so thin—I AM

80

dreadful thin, ain't I? There isn't a pick on my bones. I do love to imagine I'm nice and plump, with dimples in my elbows.

16. What is the main idea of the passage?
    a. The girl is an orphan.
    b. The girl has been in an orphanage.
    c. The girl is excited and imaginative.
    d. The girl in the orphanage is the daughter of an earl.

17. Which statement is not a detail from the passage?
    a. The child has an old carpet-bag.
    b. The child loves driving.
    c. The child is thin.
    d. The asylum was a horrible place.

18. What is the meaning of asylum in the paragraph?
    a. Hospital
    b. Sanitarium
    c. Orphanage
    d. Prison

19. What is the author's primary purpose in writing this passage?
    a. To illustrate the child's excitement.
    b. To educate the reader.
    c. To explain why orphanages were bad.
    d. To create the setting.

20. Which is the best summary of this passage?
    a. The child is frightened of the changes in her life.
    b. The child is excited by the changes in her life.
    c. The family is unhappy about the child.
    d. The family is happy about the child.

Reading Comprehension Practice Test – Answers

1. B
2. A
3. D
4. A
5. A
6. C
7. B
8. A
9. C
10. A
11. A
12. C
13. C
14. B
15. B
16. C
17. D
18. C
19. A
20. B

Chapter 6: Mathematics Skills Test

The Math Skills Test section tests various concepts in numbers and operations, algebra, geometry, data analysis, statistics, and probability. In this test section, you will be provided 40 minutes to answer a varying number of questions. This is an adaptive test section, so the number of questions you answer depends on whether you answered previous questions correctly or not. Do NOT guess on questions unless you absolutely are stuck, and even then do your best to eliminate wrong choices first. Before taking the SIFT, you want to make sure that you have a good understanding of the math areas covered. You will need to sharpen your skills, but don't worry – we'll provide you with the knowledge that you'll need to know for the test. We have 50 practice questions, which will give you an opportunity to hone your skills on the different concepts. Remember to take your time, accuracy is paramount on the Math Skills Test since you cannot go back and change answers!

Math Concepts Tested

You have a much better chance of getting a good Math Skills score if you know what to expect. The test covers math up to and including the first semester of Algebra II as well as fundamental geometry. You will not be given any formulas, such as those required for geometry calculations, so you need to make sure that you have studied them so they are fresh in your mind.

Here is a breakdown of areas covered:

Numbers and Operations
Absolute values, inequalities, probabilities, exponents, and radicals.

Algebra and Functions
Basic equation solving, simultaneous equations, binomials & polynomials, and inequalities.

Geometry and Measurement
Angle relationships, area and perimeter of geometric shapes, and volume.

Math skills that you won't need:
- Working with bulky numbers or endless calculations.
- Working with imaginary numbers or the square roots of negative numbers.
- Trigonometry or calculus.

Important Note: You are not allowed to use a calculator for any section of the AFOQT.

The Most Common Mistakes

Here is a list of the four most commonly- made mistakes concerning mathematics, starting with the most common.

1. Answer is the wrong sign (positive / negative).
2. Order of Operations not following when solving.
3. Misplaced decimal.
4. Solution is not what the question asked for.

These are the basics that individuals tend to overlook when they only have a minute or less to do their calculations. This is why it is so important that you pay attention right from the start of the problem. You may be thinking, "But, those are just common sense." Exactly! Remember, even simple mistakes still result in an incorrect answer.

Strategies

Review the Basics: First and foremost, practice your basic skills such as sign changes, order of operations, simplifying fractions, and equation manipulation. These are the skills you will use the most on almost every problem on the Math Knowledge and the Arithmetic tests sections. Remember when it comes right down to it, there are still only four math operations used to solve any math problem, which are adding, subtracting, multiplying and dividing; the only thing that changes is the order they are used to solve the problem.

Although accuracy counts more than speed; **Don't Waste Time** stuck on a question! Remember, you only have 22 minutes to answer 25 questions for this section test. This is why your knowledge of the basics is so important. If you have to stop and think about what 9 * 6 equals, or use your fingers to add 13 + 8, then you need to spend time on these fundamentals before going on to the concepts. There are minute tests at the end of this chapter. If you can complete those tests in the time specified, the time required for you to calculate the more complex problems during the test will decrease greatly.

Make an Educated Guess: If necessary, eliminate at least one answer choice as most probably incorrect and guess which one is most likely correct from the remaining choices.

Math Formulas, Facts, and Terms that You Need to Know

The next few pages will cover the various math subjects (starting with the basics, but in no particular order) along with worked examples. Use this guide to determine the areas in which you need more review and work these areas first. You should take your time at first and let your brain recall the math necessary to solve the problems, using the examples given to remember these skills.

Order of Operations

PEMDAS – **P**arentheses/**E**xponents/**M**ultiply/**D**ivide/**A**dd/**S**ubtract
Perform the operations within parentheses first, and then any exponents. After those steps, perform all multiplication and division. (These are done from left to right, as they appear in the problem) Finally, do all required addition and subtraction, also from left to right as they appear in the problem.

Example: Solve $(-(2)^2 - (4 + 7))$.
$(-4 - 11) = -15$.

Example: Solve $((5)^2 \div 5 + 4 * 2)$.
$25 \div 5 + 4 * 2$.

$5 + 8 = 13$.

Positive & Negative Number Rules

$(+) + (-) =$ Subtract the two numbers. Solution gets the sign of the larger number.

$(-) + (-) =$ Negative number.

$(-) * (-) =$ Positive number.

$(-) * (+) =$ Negative number.

$(-) / (-) =$ Positive number.

$(-) / (+) =$ Negative number.

Greatest Common Factor (GCF)

The greatest factor that divides two numbers.

Example: The GCF of 24 and 18 is 6. 6 is the largest number, or greatest factor, that can divide both 24 and 18.

Geometric Sequence

Each term is equal to the previous term multiplied by x.

Example: 2, 4, 8, 16.

$x = 2$.

Fractions

Adding and subtracting fractions requires a common denominator.

Find a common denominator for:

$$\frac{2}{3} - \frac{1}{5}$$

$$\frac{2}{3} - \frac{1}{5} = \frac{2}{3}\left(\frac{5}{5}\right) - \frac{1}{5}\left(\frac{3}{3}\right) = \frac{10}{15} - \frac{3}{15} = \frac{7}{15}$$

To add mixed fractions, work first the whole numbers, and then the fractions.

$$2\frac{1}{4} + 1\frac{3}{4} = 3\frac{4}{4} = \mathbf{4}$$

To subtract mixed fractions, convert to single fractions by multiplying the whole number by the denominator and adding the numerator. Then work as above.

$$2\frac{1}{4} - 1\frac{3}{4} = \frac{9}{4} - \frac{7}{4} = \frac{2}{4} = \mathbf{\frac{1}{2}}$$

To multiply fractions, convert any mixed fractions into single fractions and multiply across; reduce to lowest terms if needed.

$$2\frac{1}{4} * 1\frac{3}{4} = \frac{9}{4} * \frac{7}{4} = \frac{63}{16} = \mathbf{3\frac{15}{16}}$$

To divide fractions, convert any mixed fractions into single fractions, flip the second fraction, and then multiply across.

$$2\frac{1}{4} \div 1\frac{3}{4} = \frac{9}{4} \div \frac{7}{4} = \frac{9}{4} * \frac{4}{7} = \frac{36}{28} = 1\frac{8}{28} = \mathbf{1\frac{2}{7}}$$

Probabilities

A probability is found by dividing the number of desired outcomes by the number of possible outcomes. (The piece divided by the whole.)

Example: What is the probability of picking a blue marble if 3 of the 15 marbles are blue?

3/15 = 1/5. The probability is **1 in 5** that a blue marble is picked.

Prime Factorization

Expand to prime number factors.

Example: 104 = 2 * 2 * 2 * 13.

Absolute Value

The absolute value of a number is its distance from zero, not its value.

So in $|x| = a$, "x" will equal "$-a$" as well as "a."

Likewise, $|3| = 3$, and $|-3| = 3$.

Equations with absolute values will have two answers. Solve each absolute value possibility separately. All solutions must be checked into the original equation.

> **Example:** Solve for x:
> $|2x - 3| = x + 1$.
>
> Equation One: $2x - 3 = -(x + 1)$.
> $\quad\quad\quad\quad 2x - 3 = -x - 1$.
> $\quad\quad\quad\quad 3x = 2$.
> $\quad\quad\quad\quad x = 2/3$.
>
> Equation Two: $2x - 3 = x + 1$.
> $\quad\quad\quad\quad x = 4$.

Mean, Median, Mode

Mean is a math term for "average." Total all terms and divide by the number of terms.

> Find the mean of 24, 27, and 18.
> $24 + 27 + 18 = 69 \div 3 = 23$.

Median is the middle number of a given set, found after the numbers have all been put in numerical order. In the case of a set of even numbers, the middle two numbers are averaged.

> What is the median of 24, 27, and 18?
> 18, **24**, 27.
>
> What is the median of 24, 27, 18, and 19?
>
> 18, 19, 24, 27 ($19 + 24 = 43$. $43/2 = 21.5$).

Mode is the number which occurs most frequently within a given set.

> What is the mode of 2, 5, 4, 4, 3, 2, 8, 9, 2, 7, 2, and 2?
>
> The mode would be **2** because it appears the most within the set.

Exponent Rules

Rule	Example
$x^0 = 1$	$5^0 = 1$
$x^1 = x$	$5^1 = 5$
$x^a \cdot x^b = x^{a+b}$	$5^2 * 5^3 = 5^5$
$(xy)^a = x^a y^a$	$(5 * 6)^2 = 5^2 * 6^2 = 25 * 36$
$(x^a)^b = x^{ab}$	$(5^2)^3 = 5^6$
$(x/y)^a = x^a/y^a$	$(10/5)^2 = 10^2/5^2 = 100/25$
$x^a/y^b = x^{a-b}$	$5^4/5^3 = 5^1 = 5$ (remember $x \neq 0$)
$x^{1/a} = \sqrt[a]{x}$	$25^{1/2} = \sqrt[2]{25} = 5$
$x^{-a} = \dfrac{1}{x^a}$	$5^{-2} = \dfrac{1}{5^2} = \dfrac{1}{25}$ (remember $x \neq 0$)
$(-x)^a$ = positive number if "a" is even; negative number if "a" is odd.	

Roots

Root of a Product: $\sqrt[n]{a \cdot b} = \sqrt[n]{a} \cdot \sqrt[n]{b}$

Root of a Quotient: $\sqrt[n]{\dfrac{a}{b}} = \dfrac{\sqrt[n]{a}}{\sqrt[n]{b}}$

Fractional Exponent: $\sqrt[n]{a^m} = a^{m/n}$

Literal Equations

Equations with more than one variable. Solve in terms of one variable first.

Example: Solve for y: $4x + 3y = 3x + 2y$.

Step 1 – Combine like terms: $3y - 2y = 4x - 2x$.

Step 2 – Solve for y: $y = 2x$.

Midpoint

To determine the midpoint between two points, simply add the two x coordinates together and divide by 2 (midpoint x). Then add the y coordinates together and divide by 2 (midpoint y).

$$\left(\frac{x_1 + x_2}{2} , \frac{y_1 + y}{2} \right)$$

Inequalities

Inequalities are solved like linear and algebraic equations, except the sign must be reversed when dividing by a negative number.

Example: $-7x + 2 < 6 - 5x$.

Step 1 – Combine like terms: $-2x < 4$.

Step 2 – Solve for x. (Reverse the sign): $x > -2$.

Solving compound inequalities will give you two answers.

Example: $-4 \leq 2x - 2 \leq 6$.

Step 1 – Add 2 to each term to isolate x: $-2 \leq 2x \leq 8$.

Step 2: Divide by 2: $-1 \leq x \leq 4$.

Solution set is **[-1, 4]**.

Algebraic Equations

When simplifying or solving algebraic equations, you need to be able to utilize all math rules: exponents, roots, negatives, order of operations, etc.

1. Add & Subtract: Only the coefficients of like terms.

   Example: $5xy + 7y + 2yz + 11xy - 5yz = 16xy + 7y - 3yz$.

2. Multiplication: First the coefficients then the variables.

   Example: Monomial * Monomial.

   $(3x^4y^2z)(2y^4z^5) = 6x^4y^6z^6$.

   (A variable with no exponent has an implied exponent of 1.)

   Example: Monomial * Polynomial.

   $(2y^2)(y^3 + 2xy^2z + 4z) = 2y^5 + 4xy^4z + 8y^2z$.

Example: Binomial * Binomial.

$(5x + 2)(3x + 3)$.

First: $5x * 3x = 15x^2$.

Outer: $5x * 3 = 15x$.

Inner: $2 * 3x = 6x$.

Last: $2 * 3 = 6$.

Combine like terms: $15x^2 + 21x + 6$.

Example: Binomial * Polynomial.

$(x + 3)(2x^2 - 5x - 2)$.

First term: $x(2x^2 - 5x - 2) = 2x^3 - 5x^2 - 2x$.

Second term: $3(2x^2 - 5x - 2) = 6x^2 - 15x - 6$.

Added Together: $2x^3 + x^2 - 17x - 6$.

Distributive Property

When a variable is placed outside of a parenthetical set, it is *distributed* to all of the variables within that set.

$5(2y - 3x) = 10y - 15x$ [Can also be written as $(2y - 3x)5$].

$2x(3y + 1) + 6x = 6xy + 2x + 6x = 6xy + 8x$.

Fundamental Counting Principle

(The number of possibilities of an event happening) * (the number of possibilities of another event happening) = the total number of possibilities.

Example: If you take a multiple choice test with 5 questions, with 4 answer choices for each question, how many test result possibilities are there?

Solution: Question 1 has 4 choices; question 2 has 4 choices; etc.

$4 * 4 * 4 * 4 * 4$ (one for each question) = **1024 possible test results**.

Linear Systems

There are two different methods can be used to solve multiple equation linear systems:

Substitution Method: This solves for one variable in one equation and substitutes it into the other equation. **Example**: Solve: $3y - 4 + x = 0$ and $5x + 6y = 11$.

1. Step 1: Solve for one variable:
    $3y - 4 = 0$.
    $3y + x = 4$.
    $x = 4 - 3y$.

2. Step 2: Substitute into the second equation and solve:
    $5(4 - 3y) + 6y = 11$.
    $20 - 15y + 6y = 11$.
    $20 - 9y = 11$.
    $-9y = -9$.
    $y = 1$.

3. Step 3: Substitute into the first equation:
    $3(1) - 4 + x = 0$.
    $-1 + x = 0$.
    $x = 1$.

    Solution: $x = 1, y = 1$.

Addition Method: Manipulate one of the equations so that when it is added to the other, one variable is eliminated. **Example**: Solve: $2x + 4y = 8$ and $4x + 2y = 10$.

1. Step 1: Manipulate one equation to eliminate a variable when added together: $-2(2x + 4y = 8)$.
    $-4x - 8y = -16$.
    $(-4x - 8y = -16) + (4x + 2y = 10)$.
    $-6y = -6$.
    $y = 1$.

2. Step 2: Plug into an equation to solve for the other variable:
    $2x + 4(1) = 8$.
    $2x + 4 = 8$.
    $2x = 4$.
    $x = 2$.

    Solution: $x = 2, y = 1$.

Quadratics

Factoring: Converting $ax^2 + bx + c$ to factored form. Find two numbers that are factors of c and whose sum is b. **Example**: Factor: $2x^2 + 12x + 18 = 0$.

1. Step 1: If possible, factor out a common monomial: $2(x^2 - 6x + 9)$.

2. Step 2: Find two numbers that are factors of 9 and which equal -6 when added:
   $2(x\ \ )(x\ \ )$.
       -3 , -3

3. Step 3: Fill in the binomials. Be sure to check your answer signs.
   $2(x - 3)(x - 3)$.

4. Step 4: To solve, set each to equal 0.
   $x - 3 = 0$. So, $x = 3$.

Difference of squares:

$a^2 - b^2 = (a + b)(a - b)$.

$a^2 + 2ab + b^2 = (a + b)(a + b)$.

$a^2 - 2ab + b^2 = (a - b)(a - b)$.

Geometry

- **Acute Angle**: Measures less than 90°.

- **Acute Triangle**: Each angle measures less than 90°.

- **Obtuse Angle**: Measures greater than 90°.

- **Obtuse Triangle**: One angle measures greater than 90°.

- **Adjacent Angles**: Share a side and a vertex.

- **Complementary Angles**: Adjacent angles that sum to 90°.

- **Supplementary Angles**: Adjacent angles that sum to 180°.

- **Vertical Angles**: Angles that are opposite of each other. They are always congruent (equal in measure).

- **Equilateral Triangle**: All angles are equal.

- **Isosceles Triangle**: Two sides and two angles are equal.

- **Scalene**: No equal angles.

- **Parallel Lines**: Lines that will never intersect. Y **ll** X means line Y is parallel to line X.

- **Perpendicular Lines**: Lines that intersect or cross to form 90° angles.

- **Transversal Line**: A line that crosses parallel lines.

- **Bisector**: Any line that cuts a line segment, angle, or polygon exactly in half.

- **Polygon**: Any enclosed plane shape with three or more connecting sides (ex. a triangle).

- **Regular Polygon**: Has all equal sides and equal angles (ex. square).

- **Arc**: A portion of a circle's edge.

- **Chord**: A line segment that connects two different points on a circle.

- **Tangent**: Something that touches a circle at only one point without crossing through it.

- **Sum of Angles**: The sum of angles of a polygon can be calculated using $(n-1)180°$, when n = the number of sides.

Regular Polygons

Polygon Angle Principle: S = The sum of interior angles of a polygon with n-sides.

$S = (n-2)180.$

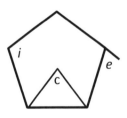

The measure of each central angle (c) is $360°/n$.
The measure of each interior angle (i) is $(n-2)180°/n$.
The measure of each exterior angle (e) is $360°/n$.
To compare areas of similar polygons: $A_1/A_2 = (side_1/side_2)^2$.

Triangles

The angles in a triangle add up to 180°.

Area of a triangle = ½ * *b* * *h*, or ½*bh*.

Pythagoras' Theorem: $a^2 + b^2 = c^2$.

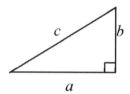

Trapezoids

Four-sided polygon, in which the bases (and only the bases) are parallel.
Isosceles Trapezoid – base angles are congruent.

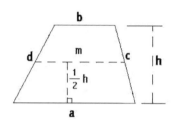

Area and Perimeter of a Trapezoid

$$m = \frac{1}{2}(a + b)$$

$$Area = \frac{1}{2}h * (a + b) = m * h$$

$$Perimeter = a + b + c + d = 2m + c + d$$

If *m* is the median then: $m \parallel \overline{AB}$ and $m \parallel CD$

Rhombus

Four-sided polygon, in which all four sides are congruent and opposite sides are parallel.

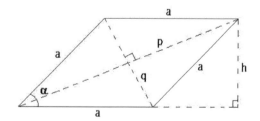

Area and Perimeter of a Rhombus

$$Perimeter = 4a$$

$$Area = a^2 \sin \alpha = a * h = \frac{1}{2}pq$$

$$4a^2 = p^2 + q^2$$

Rectangle

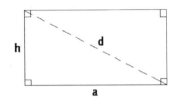

Area and Perimeter of a Rectangle

$$d = \sqrt{a^2 + h^2}$$

$$a = \sqrt{d^2 - h^2}$$

$$h = \sqrt{d^2 - a^2}$$

$$Perimeter = 2a + 2h$$

$$Area = a \cdot h$$

Square

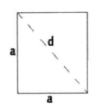

Area and Perimeter of a Square

$$d = a\sqrt{2}$$

$$Perimeter = 4a = 2d\sqrt{2}$$

$$Area = a^2 = \frac{1}{2}d^2$$

Circle

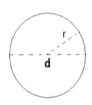

Area and Perimeter of a Circle

$$d = 2r$$

$$Perimeter = 2\pi r = \pi d$$

$$Area = \pi r^2$$

Cube

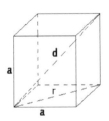

Area and Volume of a Cube

$$r = a\sqrt{2}$$

$$d = a\sqrt{3}$$

$$Area = 6a^2$$

$$Volume = a^3$$

Cuboid

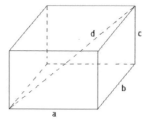

Area and Volume of a Cuboid

$$d = \sqrt{a^2 + b^2 + c^2}$$

$$A = 2(ab + ac + bc)$$

$$V = abc$$

Cylinder

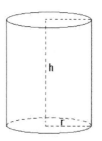

Area and Volume of a Cylinder

$$d = 2r$$

$$A_{surface} = 2\pi rh$$

$$A_{base} = 2\pi r^2$$

$$Area = A_{surface} + A_{base}$$

$$= 2\pi r (h + r)$$

$$Volume = \pi r^2 h$$

Solving Word Problems

Any of the math concepts discussed here can be turned into a word problem, and you'll likely see word problems in various forms throughout the test.

The most important step in solving any word problem is to read the entire problem before beginning to solve it: one of the most commonly made mistakes on word problems is providing an answer to a question that wasn't asked. Also, remember that not all of the information given in a problem is always needed to solve it.

When working multiple-choice word problems like those on the SIFT, it's important to check your answer. Many of the incorrect choices will be answers that test-takers arrive at by making common mistakes. So even if an answer you calculated is a given as an answer choice, that doesn't necessarily mean you've worked the problem correctly—you have to check your own work to make sure.

General Steps for Word Problem Solving

Step 1: Read the entire problem and determine what the question is asking for.

Step 2: List all of the given data and define the variables.

Step 3: Determine the formula(s) needed or set up equations from the information in the problem.

Step 4: Solve.

Step 5: Check your answer. (Is the amount too large or small? Are the answers in the correct unit of measure?)

Key Words

Word problems generally contain key words that can help you determine what math processes may be required in order to solve them.

Addition: added, combined, increased by, in all, total, perimeter, sum, and more than

Subtraction: how much more, less than, fewer than, exceeds, difference, and decreased

Multiplication: of, times, area, and product

Division: distribute, share, average, per, out of, percent, and quotient

Equals: is, was, are, amounts to, and were

Basic Word Problems

A word problem in algebra is just an equation or a set of equations described using words. Your task when solving these problems is to turn the "story" of the problem into mathematical equations.

Examples
1)   A store owner bought a case of 48 backpacks for $476.00. He sold 17 of the backpacks in his store for $18 each, and the rest were sold to a school for $15 each. What was the salesman's profit?

Answer:
Start by listing all the data and defining the variable:
total number of backpacks = 48
cost of backpacks = $476.00
backpacks sold in store at price of $18 = 17
backpacks sold to school at a price of $15 = 75 − 17 = 58
total profit = x

Now set up an equation:

$$total\ profit\ =\ income\ -\ cost$$
$$x = [(17 \times 18) + (58 \times 15)] - 476$$
$$x = 1176 - 476 = 700$$

The store owner made a profit of **$700**.

2)   Thirty students in Mr. Joyce's room are working on projects over 2 days. The first day, he gave them 3/5 hour to work. On the second day, he gave them half as much time as the first day. How much time did each student have to work on the project?

Answer:
Start by listing all the data and defining your variables. Note that the number of students, while given in the problem, is not needed to find the answer:

time on 1st day $= \frac{3}{5}$ hr. $= 36$ min.

time on 2nd day $= \frac{1}{2}(36) = 18$ min.

total time $= x$

Now set up the equation and solve:
$$total\ time\ =\ time\ on\ 1st\ day\ +\ time\ on\ 2nd\ day$$
$$x = 36 + 18 = 54$$

The students had **54 minutes** to work on the projects.

Distance Word Problems
Distance word problems involve something traveling at a constant or average speed. Whenever you read a problem that involves *how fast*, *how far*, or *for how long*, you should think of the distance equation, $d = rt$, where d stands for distance, r for rate (speed), and t for time.

These problems can be solved by setting up a grid with d, r, and t along the top and each moving object on the left. When setting up the grid, make sure the units are consistent. For example, if the distance is in meters and the time is in seconds, the rate should be meters per second.

<u>Examples</u>
1)   Will drove from his home to the airport at an average speed of 30 mph. He then boarded a helicopter and flew to the hospital with an average speed of 60 mph. The entire distance was 150 miles, and the trip took 3 hours. Find the distance from the airport to the hospital.

Answer:
The first step is to set up a table and fill in a value for each variable:

	d	r	t
driving	d	30	t

98

flying	$150 - d$	60	$3 - t$

You can now set up equations for driving and flying. The first row gives the equation $d = 30t$, and the second row gives the equation $150 - d = 60(3 - t)$.

Next, you can solve this system of equations. Start by substituting for d in the second equation:

$d = 30t$
$150 - d = 60(30 - t) \rightarrow 150 - 30t = 60(30 - t)$
Now solve for t:
$150 - 30t = 180 - 60t$
$-30 = -30t$
$1 = t$

Although you've solved for t, you're not done yet. Notice that the problem asks for distance. So, you need to solve for d: what the problem asked for. It does not ask for time, but the time is needed to solve the problem.

Driving: $30t = 30$ miles
Flying: $150 - d = 120$ miles
The distance from the airport to the hospital is **120 miles**.

2)   Two riders on horseback start at the same time from opposite ends of a field that is 45 miles long. One horse is moving at 14 mph and the second horse is moving at 16 mph. How long after they begin will they meet?

Answer:
First, set up the table. The variable for time will be the same for each, because they will have been on the road for the same amount of time when they meet:

	d	r	t
Cyclist #1	d	14	t
Cyclist #2	$45 - d$	16	t

Nest set up two equations:

Horse #1: $d = 14t$
Horse #2: $45 - d = 16t$
Now substitute and solve:
$d = 14t$
$45 - d = 16t \rightarrow 45 - 14t = 16t$
$45 = 30t$
$t = 1.5$

They will meet **1.5 hr.** after they begin.

99

Work Problems

Work problems involve situations where several people or machines are doing work at different rates. Your task is usually to figure out how long it will take these people or machines to complete a task while working together. The trick to doing work problems is to figure out how much of the project each person or machine completes in the same unit of time. For example, you might calculate how much of a wall a person can paint in 1 hour, or how many boxes an assembly line can pack in 1 minute.

Once you know that, you can set up an equation to solve for the total time. This equation usually has a form similar to the equation for distance, but here *work = rate × time*.

<u>Examples</u>

1)   Hayden can clean an entire house in 12 hours while his sister Jo takes 8 hours. How long would it take for Hayden and Jo to clean 2 houses together?

Answer:

Start by figuring out how much of a house each sibling can clean on his or her own. Hayden can clean the house in 12 hours, so he can clean $\frac{1}{12}$ of the house in an hour. Using the same logic, Jo can clean $\frac{1}{8}$ of a house in a hour.

By adding these values together, you get the fraction of the house they can clean together in an hour:

$$\frac{1}{12} + \frac{1}{8} = \frac{5}{24}$$

They can do $\frac{5}{24}$ of the job per hour.

Now set up variables and an equation to solve:

t = time spent cleaning (in hours)
h = number of houses cleaned = 2

work = rate × time
$$h = \frac{5}{24}t \rightarrow$$
$$2 = \frac{5}{24}t \rightarrow$$
$$t = \frac{48}{5} = 9\frac{3}{5}\textbf{hr.}$$

2) Farmer Dan needs to water his corn field. One hose can water a field 1.25 times faster than a second pipe. When both hoses are running, they water the field in 5 hours. How long would it take to water the field if only the slower hose is used?

Answer:
In this problem you don't know the exact time, but you can still find the hourly rate as a variable:

The second hose completes the job in f hours, so it waters $\frac{1}{f}$ field per hour. The faster hose waters the field in $1.25f$, so it waters the field in $\frac{1}{1.25f}$ hours. Together, they take 5 hours to water the field, so they water $\frac{1}{5}$ of the field per hour.

Now you can set up the equations and solve:
$$\frac{1}{f} + \frac{1}{1.25f} = \frac{1}{5} \rightarrow$$
$$1.25f\left(\frac{1}{f} + \frac{1}{1.25f}\right) = 1.25f\left(\frac{1}{5}\right) \rightarrow$$
$$1.25 + 1 = 0.25f$$
$$2.25 = 0.25f$$
$$f = 9$$

The slow hose takes 9 hours to water the field. The fast hose takes $1.25(9) = \mathbf{11.25\ hours}$.

3) Martha takes 2 hours to pluck 500 apples, and George takes 3 hours to pluck 450 apples. How long will they take, working together, to pluck 1000 apples?

Answer:
Calculate how many apples each person can pluck per hour:

Ben: $\dfrac{500\ \text{apples}}{2\ \text{hr.}} = \dfrac{250\ \text{apples}}{\text{hr.}}$

Frank: $\dfrac{450\ \text{apples}}{3\ \text{hr.}} = \dfrac{150\ \text{apples}}{\text{hr.}}$

Together: $\dfrac{(250 + 150)\ \text{apples}}{\text{hr}} = \dfrac{400\ \text{apples}}{\text{hr.}}$

Now set up an equation to find the time it takes to pick 1000 apples:
$$total\ time = \frac{1\ \text{hr.}}{400\ \text{apples}} \times 1000\ \text{apples} = \frac{1000}{400}\ \text{hr.} = \mathbf{2.5\ hr.}$$

Mathematics Knowledge Practice Test

1. Which of these are parallel lines?
A. x=2, y=3
B. y=-1, x=4
C. x=1, x=6
D. x=9, y=100

2. Which of these are complementary angles?
A. 63° and 29°
B. 56° and 38°
C. 33° and 57°
D. 46° and 49°

3. The triangle whose one angle is greater than 90 degrees is called …
A. Equilateral Triangle
B. Isosceles Triangle
C. Scalene Triangle
D. Obtuse Triangle

4. a×(b+c) = …
A. ab+bc
B. cb+ac
C. ab+ac
D. abc

5. Which of the following options is true for Equilateral Triangle?
A. Three Congruent Angles
B. Three Congruent Sides
C. Two Congruent Angles
D. Two Congruent Sides

6. If (20-x)/4=3y. What will be x in terms on y?
A. 20-12y
B. 20+12y
C. 12-20y
D. 12+20y

7. If 38 is divided by m then the remainder is 2 and the quotient is 12. What will be the value of "m" then?
A. 2
B. 3
C. 5
D. 4

8. If $y = 7x$, $x = 3z$. What will be the value of y if $z = 2$?

A. 40

B. 44

C. 48

D. 42

9. $4\ 4/6 + 2\ 1/3 - 1\ 3/4 \times 3\ 2/5 = \ldots$

A. 22/20

B. 24/20

C. 21/20

D. 25/20

10. Which one of the following options shows the correct answer of y with respect to its equation?

A. If $2(y-1)+6=0$, then $y=2$

B. If $3(y-3)=3$, then $y=4$

C. If $2(y+2)=6$, then $y=-1$

D. If $6y-18 = 6$, then $y=5$

11. $A = x2+3x-4$, $B = 2x2-2x+3$. What will be the value of "B-A"?

A. x2-5x+7

B. 3x2-x-1

C. x2-3x+7

D. x2-5x-7

12. Pythagorean Theorem is applicable to which one of the following triangles?

A. Equilateral Triangle

B. Acute Triangle

C. Obtuse Triangle

D. Right-Angled Triangle

13. $x=3$ is the solution of which one of the following equations?

A. $6(x+3)-12 = 0$

B. $8(x-2)-4 = 0$

C. $7(x-6)+21 = 0$

D. $3(x+4)-9 = 0$

14. There are two parallel lines x and y. One line s is passing through both these parallel lines such that $<smx = 60°$. What will be the value of angle x?

A. 120°

B. 60°

C. 80°

D. 150°

15. What will be the product of 3p3-2p2+p and -2p will give?
A. -6p4+4p3-2p2
B. 6p4-4p3+2p2
C. -6p3+4p2-2p
D. 6p4+4p3-2p2

16. We have two numbers x and y such that x+y=15, x-y=3. What will be the numbers?
A. x=8, y=5
B. x=10, y=7
C. x=8, y=7
D. x=9, y=6

17. Allison collects 300 plastic bottles in week one, 420 plastic bottles in week two, and 180 plastic bottles in the last week for recycling. Plastic bottles can be traded for reusable tote bags. If 25 plastic bottles earn her one tote bag, how many tote bags can Allison collect?
A.   36
B.   50
C.   20
D.   25

18. Grendel is 10 years older than Freddie, who is 16. How old is Grendel?
A.   26
B.   30
C.   36
D.   25

19. Josh and Jeff got summer jobs at the local burger joint. They were each supposed to work 15 hours per week for two months. During that time, Jeff went on a family vacation for one week and Josh took his shifts. How many hours in total did Josh work during these eight weeks?
A.   120 hours
B.   135 hours
C.   150 hours
D.   185 hours

20. A shirt originally priced at $40 is on sale for $30. What percent has the shirt been discounted?
A.   25%
B.   33%
C.   70%
D.   75%

21. If Lobelia purchases an item that costs $30 or less, she will pay with cash. If Lobelia purchases an item that costs between $30 and $70, she will pay with a check. If Lobelia purchases an item that costs $70 or greater, she will use a credit card. If Lobelia recently made a payment for a certain item through check, which of the following statements could be true?
A. The item cost $80.
B. If the item had cost $20 more, she would have paid with cash.
C. The item cost at least $70.
D. The item cost more than $25.

22. Which of the options given best represents the following sentence? Carmen (C) had three apples and ate one.
A. $C = 3 - 1$
B. $3 - 2 = C$
C. $C = 3 \times 2$
D. $3C - 2$

23. If there is 0.125 of a pint in a gallon, how many pints are in 3.5 gallons of ice cream?
A. 27.725
B. 25
C. 26.125
D. 28

24. Carpet costs $2.89 per square foot. What would be the cost to carpet a bedroom whose dimensions are 4 yards by 5 yards?
A. $570.80
B. $730.40
C. $289.00
D. $520.20

25. 4/13 of Abigail's paycheck goes to her cell phone bill. If the amount of her paycheck towards her cell phone bill is $26.80, what is the amount of her total paycheck?
A. $8.25
B. $82.50
C. $87.10
D. $348.40

26. A car driving at a constant speed leaves Houston, Texas for Fort Halifax, Maine (at time t = 0). If Fort Halifax is 2,000 miles from Houston, which option offers the best equation for distance (D) from Fort Halifax at any time, t?
A. $D(t) = 60t - 2,000$
B. $D(t) = 60t$
C. $D(t) = 2,000 - 60t$
D. $D(t) = 2,000 + 60t$

27. A company decided to let their employees select their new logo via vote. The new logo was selected with 60% of the votes cast. Only 50% of the company's 35,000 employees voted. How many votes did the new logo receive?
A. 7,500
B. 10,500
C. 17,500
D. 21,000

28. John is 5 feet 11 inches tall, and Peter is 6 feet 5 inches tall. How much taller is Peter than John?
A. 1 foot 7 inches
B. 1 foot
C. 7 inches
D. 6 inches

29. How many 32-passenger buses will it take to carry 192 people?
A. 6
B. 5
C. 7
D. 3

30. If 1/3 of a 12-inch ruler is broken off, how much is left behind in inches?
A. 4 inches
B. 3 inches
C. 8 inches
D. 6 inches

31. A zoo pays $0.12 per pound every day to feed a 2-ton rhinoceros. How much does it cost to feed the rhinoceros every day?
A. $480
B. $240
C. $120
D. $600

32. A landscaping company charges 5 cents per square foot for the application of fertilizer. How much would they ask for to fertilize a 30 foot by 50 foot lawn?
A. $7.50
B. $15.00
C. $75.00
D. $150.00

33. What is the volume of a cube whose width is 5 inches?
A. 15 cubic inches
B. 25 cubic inches
C. 64 cubic inches
D. 125 cubic inches

34. (|2k+4|)/8=2 Which of the following values of 'k' satisfies this equation?
A. (12, 2)
B. (4, 5)
C. (3, 6)
D. (-10, 6)

35. If (2x+7)/9 < 2, which of the following options is correct?
A. 3x < 21/3
B. x > -3
C. x < 11/2
D. 2x > 1

36. What is the result when we multiply these given fractions?
4/5*14/25*125/7*4/2
A. 16
B. 24/25
C. 32
D. 18

37. What is the result when we multiply these given fractions?
2/9*3/25*125/6*3/10
A. 6/30
B. 1/6
C. 6
D. 11/30

38. What is the result when we add these given fractions?
1/5+4/25=_____
A. 8/25
B. 5/29
C. 9/25
D. 5/20

39. If 3x + 2 > 5, which of the following options is correct?
A. x <1
B. x >-1
C. x >1
D. x >3

40. What is the median of the following list of numbers: 4, 5, 7, 9, 10, and 12?
A. 6
B. 7.5
C. 7.8
D. 8

41. If 4x-12 < 12, which of the following options is correct?
A. 2x <12
B. x >12
C. x >11
D. x >21

42. The sales price of a truck is $14,590, which is 20% off the original price. What is the original price?
A. $17,310.40
B. $16,990.90
C. $15,290.70
D. $18,237.50

43. If a discount of 25% off the retail price of a pair of shoes saves Jacqueline $45, what was the shoes' original price?
A. $125
B. $165
C. $180
D. $200

44. Nick needs to purchase a study guide for a test. The study guide costs $80.00, and the sales tax is 8.25%. Nick has $100. How much change will Nick receive back?
A. $6.20
B. $7.45
C. $13.40
D. $19.85

45. Molly's headband broke and her hair is falling in her face. She has 4 pieces of ribbon. She needs to choose the piece that will be able to go around her 22 inch head. The piece must be at least 4 inches longer than her head so that she can tie a knot, but it cannot be more than 6 inches so that the ends will show through her hair. Which of the following pieces of ribbon will work best?
A.   2 feet
B.   2 ¾ feet
C.   2 5/8 feet
D.   2 1/3 feet

46. Tiles are $12.51 per square yard. What will it cost to tile a room with if the room is 10 feet wide and 12 feet long?
A. $166.80
B. $178.70
C. $184.60
D. $190.90

47. Dr. Green has asked you to give Anna 20 mg of morphine. The morphine is stored as 4 mg per 5-mL dose. How many milliliters does Anna need?
A.   15 mL
B.   20 mL
C.   25 mL
D.   30 mL

48. Leslie needs to make a pie and some cupcakes. The pie requires 3/8 cup of butter, and the cupcakes require 3/5 cup of butter. Leslie has 15/16 cups of butter. Does she have enough butter, or how much more does she need?
A.   She has enough butter
B.   She needs 1/8 of a cup of butter
C.   She needs 3/80 of a cup of butter
D.   She needs 4/19 of a cup of butter

49. Alan bought a pizza that had 8 slices. Alan ate 3 slices of pizza at lunch, and left the remaining pizza for Alana. What fraction of pizza did he leave for Alana?
A.   3/8
B.   1/2
C.   4/5
D.   5/8

50. During a 5-day convention, the number of visitors tripled each day. If the convention started on a Tuesday with 345 visitors, what was the attendance on that Friday?
A.   9,31
B.   1,035
C.   1,725
D.   3,105

Math Knowledge Practice Test - Answers

1. C	26. C
2. C	27. B
3. D	28. D
4. C	29. A
5. A	30. C
6. A	31. A
7. B	32. C
8. D	33. D
9. C	34. D
10. B	35. C
11. A	36. A
12. D	37. B
13. C	38. C
14. A	39. C
15. A	40. D
16. D	41. A
17. A	42. D
18. A	43. C
19. B	44. C
20. A	45. D
21. D	46. A
22. A	47. C
23. D	48. C
24. D	49. D
25. C	50. A

Chapter 7: Mechanical Comprehension

The mechanics section of the SIFT has a 15 minute time limit, but the number of questions varies since like the Math Skills Test, it is a computer adaptive section. It is important to note again, you cannot skip any questions, nor can you come back and change any answers. It is imperative that you do your absolute best on each question, meaning that even if you have to guess, carefully eliminate as many wrong choices as possible first.

Before diving into the topics covered in the mechanical section of the SIFT, we should first define two types of values used in physics; **scalars** and **vectors**.

In most basic math, simple numerical values are calculated (for instance 1 + 1 = 2). These simple numbers are known as **scalar** values, meaning they have a magnitude, but no direction, associated with them. Mass is an example of a scalar value commonly used in physics.

However, we live in a three-dimensional universe, so normally a simple number cannot sufficiently describe a physical characteristic. Instead, we need a magnitude as well as a direction, which is known as a **vector**. A vector not only tells how large a value is, but also whether it acts upward, to the left, to the right, etc.

For example, **speed** is a scalar value that tells you how fast an object is going. But if you are driving, knowing only the speed of your car, it will be impossible to navigate. Instead, you need to know your speed as well as the direction in which you are traveling, which is a vector value known as **velocity**. Velocity tells the direction and speed that an object is traveling.

Force and Newton's Laws of Motion
A **force** is a push or pull that can result in an object's motion or change of shape, and has a magnitude and direction, making it a vector. Force is measured in **Newtons** (N) in the metric system of units, but can also be measured in the standard unit of **pounds force** (lbf).

Though its effects can be noticed, a force cannot be seen; it can be thought of as an interaction between two bodies. The basic rules of forces are described by **Newton's Laws of Motion**, which are the foundation of the field of **mechanics.**

1. **First Law of Motion**: Until acted on by an external force, an object's velocity will remain constant, meaning speed and direction will not change. You may recognize: "An object at rest will remain at rest and an object in motion will remain in motion until a force is applied." An object's natural resistance to a change in its motion is known as **inertia**, so Newton's first law is also known as the **Law of Inertia**.

   Intuitively, the law of inertia makes sense. If a soccer ball is resting in a field, it is not going to move until someone kicks it. Once the ball is kicked, though, it does not continue to travel forever, which seems like it is a violation of Newton's first law.

However, there are forces such as drag from the air and friction from the field that eventually cause the ball to come to stop again. In the same way, if a moving car is put into neutral, it will slow down and eventually stop due to parasitic losses in the car's wheels and drivetrain, aero drag, and friction.

2. **Second Law of Motion**: Describes a force's effect on the motion of a body. It states that the acceleration of the object will be proportional to the sum of the forces being applied. Algebraically, Newton's second law is written as: $F = m * a$.

   Here, F is force, m is mass in kilograms (kg) or pounds mass (lbm), and a is acceleration in meters per second squared (m/s^2) or feet per second squared (ft/s^2). Notice that force and acceleration are both vectors, so the acceleration of an object will be in the direction of the force being applied to it.

   Acceleration is defined as the rate of change of an object's velocity. Acceleration does not have to result in a change in speed; it can also cause a change in direction, as is the case in centripetal, or rotational, acceleration. Remember that velocity and acceleration are two separate and distinct values. Just because the acceleration is positive does not mean that the object's velocity is positive and vice versa.

   A negative velocity would mean the object is going backward (or opposite of the direction designated as "positive") and a positive acceleration means the object's velocity is increasing in the positive direction (or decreasing in the negative direction). Though the term "deceleration" is often used to describe a decrease in speed, this is not technically correct. Instead, a change in velocity is always called acceleration and can either be positive or negative, depending on direction.

3. **Third Law of Motion**: Involves the coupling of forces and reactions. The law is often stated as, "For every action there is an equal and opposite reaction." The actions and reactions we are considering are forces. For example, if you lean against a wall, you are applying a force on the wall. According to Newton's third law, the wall is applying the same force back on you. These two forces will be the same magnitude, but in opposite directions; you push toward the wall and the wall pushes back on you. Because there is no motion involved when you lean again a wall, this is considered a **static** example.

   A **dynamic** example of Newton's third law is two cars crashing. If one car collides into a second, stationary car, both cars feel the same amount of force. The force applied to the stationary car is in the direction of the collision and causes the car to begin moving in the same direction as the first car. The moving car would have a force applied to it in the opposite direction by the stationary car, resulting in, among other things, a decrease in speed. Since the force on the two cars will be in opposite directions, the acceleration of the cars will also be in opposite directions; the stationary car speeds up and the moving car slows down.

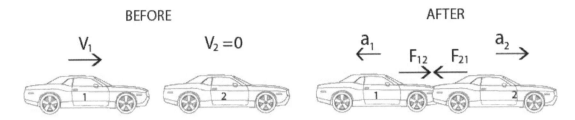

BEFORE · AFTER

Collision of a car moving at velocity V₁ into the second stationary car with the force car 1 applies on car 2 F₁, the equal force car 2 applies on car 1 F₂₁, and the resulting accelerations a₁ and a₂.

Centrifugal Force

The terms centripetal and centrifugal force are often incorrectly used interchangeably. A **centripetal force** is a force that makes an object travel along a curved path. This means a centripetal force creates a **centripetal acceleration** toward the center of the curved path.

For example, when a car is driven in a circle, the front tires exert a centripetal force on the car, accelerating it toward the center of the circle. Passengers in the car feel as though they are being pulled toward the outside of the circle, and this pull is **centrifugal acceleration**, which results from **centrifugal force**.

A centrifugal force is the reaction force of a centripetal force that pulls an object toward the outside of the curved path being traveled. This all means that a centrifugal force and a centripetal force are of equal magnitude and opposite directions, just as would be expected of a force and reaction according to Newton's third law. As Newton's second law states, centripetal force equals the mass of the object multiplied by centripetal acceleration:

$$F_c = m * a_c = m * v^2/R$$

Here, a_c is the centripetal acceleration and is equal to the square of the object's linear velocity (v) divided by the radius of the curved path, R.

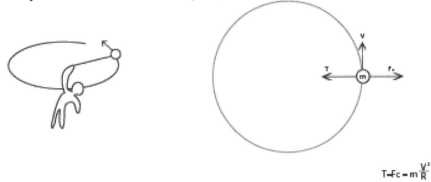

$$T = F_c = m \frac{v^2}{R}$$

When a ball on a string is swung in a circle, the string exerts a centripetal force on the ball, preventing it from leaving the circular path, and the resulting centrifugal force pulls the ball outward, causing tension in the string and keeping it taut.

The Law of Gravity and Weight

Sir Isaac Newton also formulated the **law of universal gravitation**. Although it is not considered one of Newton's three laws of motion, this is a very important law of physics and has profound implications in our world. Many people are familiar with the story of Isaac Newton observing a falling apple and coming up with the idea of gravity.

Though the authenticity of this story, and even whether Newton was the original formulator of the law, is unclear, Newton's law of universal gravitation is nonetheless named after him, and it describes the mutual attraction between celestial bodies, such as planets and stars. It states that the **gravitational force** two bodies exert on each other is proportional to their masses and inversely proportional to the square of the distance between them:

$$F_g = G * m_1 * m_2 \, r^2$$

Here, G is the **universal gravitation constant** ($6.674 * 10^{-11}$ Nm^2/kg^2), m_1 and m_2 are the masses of the two bodies, and r is the distance between them. You may notice that there is no vector on the right side of this equation. The product of scalar values cannot equal a vector because no direction is specified, so this equation is not technically correct.

This is because the right side of this equation normally has a unit vector with a length of 1 in the direction of the measurement of the distance between the two planets. This has been left out, but remember that gravity is an attractive force; it will always tend to pull two bodies toward each other with equal force.

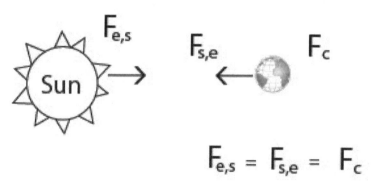

The gravitational force exerted by the sun on the Earth $F_{s,e}$ is equal to the gravitational force applied to the sun by the earth $F_{e,s}$ and is balanced (equal to) the centrifugal force resulting from the Earth's movement.

Newton's law of universal gravitation is a fairly complex concept and would seem difficult to apply to an object on the earth since there are so many objects applying a gravitational force on each other. Just look around; every object you see is applying a gravitational force on you, and you are pulling all those things toward you with the same force!

Thankfully, the law of gravity can be greatly simplified when dealing with objects on the earth's surface. The earth has a mass so much greater than any of the other objects around you that the force of gravity pulling objects toward the earth's center is much stronger than the attraction between any objects on the earth's surface. This means that we can ignore all gravitational forces besides the earth's gravity, which proves accurate when making calculations except in very rare cases, such as when a person is standing next to the Himalayan Mountains. (Next to the Himalayan Mountains, a plumb line will not point directly toward the center of the earth, but skew slightly toward the mountains, but even in this case the error in measurements is small.)

Another simplification arises from the huge radius of the earth. No matter how good of an arm you have, if you throw a ball into the air, it will not go very far at all when compared to the earth's radius. This means that even if you take an elevator to the top of a very tall building, you really haven't changed your distance from the center of the earth, so you'll still feel approximately the same gravitational force.

Therefore, we can reduce the universal gravitation equation to a simple equation for the earth's force of gravity on an object:

$$F_g = m * g$$

Here, m is the mass of the object in kilograms (kg) or pounds mass (lbm) and g is the **acceleration due to gravity**, which is 9.81 m/s^2 or 32.2 ft/s^2 towards the center of the earth. This constant acceleration of gravity near the surface of the earth means that any object, no matter what its mass, will fall to the ground at the same rate, as long as there is not significant aero drag. If a bowling ball and an orange are dropped from a building at the same time, they will accelerate toward the earth at the same rate and hit the ground at the same time.

The constant acceleration of gravity also gives rise to the concept of **weight**. The weight of an object is merely a measure of the force of gravity on the object ($m * g$), and is measured in Newtons (N) or pounds force (lbf).

The object's mass is a constant scalar value that cannot be changed. However, if the object is taken to another planet, its weight, which is a vector, may be different depending on that planet's acceleration of gravity. The fact that weight is a force means that an object, such as this book, resting on your table exerts a force on the table; the table exerts a force of the same magnitude, the object's weight, back on the object.

This force exerted back on the object opposing the object's weight is known as a **normal force** because it is normal, or perpendicular, to the surface of the table. If you hold this book flat in your hands, you must apply an upward force to keep the book stationary; therefore you are supplying the normal force equal to the book's weight.

Table Supporting the Weight of a Book

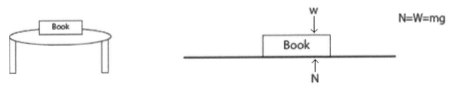

Gravity exerts a force equal to the book's weight onto the table and the table exerts an normal force back on the book so the book does not fall to the ground.

115

Another concept arising from the idea of weight force is an object's **center of gravity** or **center of mass**. The center of mass is essentially the average location of the object and is often used in physics to simplify problems, treating the object as a single particle with all of its mass at its center of gravity.

An object's stability is also determined by the location of its center of gravity. For example, if you stand flat-footed with straight legs and try to reach for an object fairly far in front of you, you may feel off-balanced. When you lean forward and reach out your arms, you are shifting your center of gravity forward in front of your feet, creating a torque that will cause you to fall forward once it is too great for your feet to overcome.

However, if you either bend your knees or stick one of your legs out behind you as you reach forward, the extra weight behind your grounded foot counteracts the weight in front of your foot so that your center of gravity does not shift, keeping you balanced.

This is very similar to a crane that has a large weight just behind the operator's cab to counteract added weight on the crane's arm when lifting. This weight's position is often adjustable, so it can be moved farther away from the crane's base when picking up objects that are either heavy or near the end of the crane's arm; without this large counterweight, a crane could not lift heavy objects without tipping over.

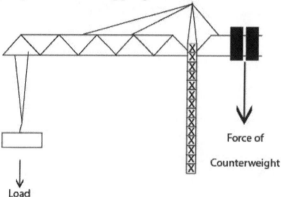

Torque
Torque (twisting force which attempts to rotate an object), or **moment** due to a force, equals the distance of the force from the **fulcrum**, or pivot point, multiplied by the tangential force: $T = F * r$.

F is the force and r is the **torque arm**, or distance from the fulcrum.

In the crane example, the middle of the crane acts as a fulcrum and the counterweight and load apply forces downward, creating two moments in opposite directions; the load is twisting the crane counterclockwise and the counterweight twists clockwise. Torque is measured in Newton-meters (Nm) or foot-pounds-force (lbf-ft).

It is important to remember that the force and distance are both vectors, which means that the component of force and the torque arm considered must be perpendicular. Applying force to the handle of a wrench is another example.

If the 10lbf force is applied to a 10-inch wrench, then the torque on the bolt is 100 in-lbf. If the force is not applied at a 90 degree angle, the resulting torque will not be as high. For instance, if the force is applied at a 30 degree angle to the wrench handle, then the component of the force perpendicular to the wrench is only 5 lbf, and the resulting torque is just 50 in-lbf.

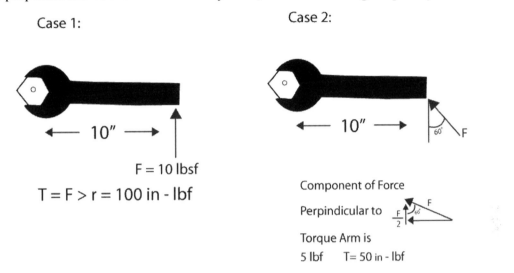

Friction

The normal force created by gravity also gives rise to a resistance to sliding known as **friction**. If you try to slide a refrigerator across a floor, you may find it very hard to move the object. Newton's third law suggests that there must be a force opposing your attempts to push the refrigerator; if not, it would easily slide across the floor and continue to slide until acted on by another force, such as a wall. This force opposing your efforts to move the refrigerator is friction. There are two types of friction: static and kinetic.

As you might have guessed, **static friction** is the force of friction between two objects that are not moving relative to each other. Static friction arises from the attempt to slide two surfaces past each other. In our refrigerator example, there is no force of friction until you attempt to push the refrigerator.

If you are not applying a force on the refrigerator, the only forces felt by the refrigerator are the force of gravity and the normal force of the floor holding it up, both of which are equal to the refrigerator's weight. When you start to push on the refrigerator and it does not move, static friction is holding the refrigerator in place.

The force of static friction is equal to the force that you are applying to the refrigerator; however, once pushed hard enough, the refrigerator will begin to move. The force necessary to start sliding an object is called **stiction** and is given by the equation: $F_{f,s} = \mu_s * N$.

$F_{f,s}$ is the maximum force of static friction (stiction), N is the normal force applied on the object by the surface across which it is sliding, and μ_s is the **coefficient of static friction**. Past this stiction point, the object will begin to move, and the force of **kinetic friction** will oppose the sliding motion: $F_{f,k} = \mu_k * N$. This is the same as the equation for static friction, except that the coefficient μ_k is the **coefficient of kinetic friction**.

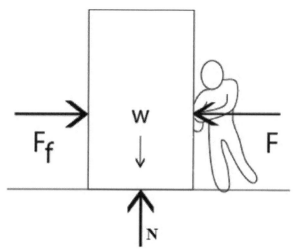

The force of friction, whether static or kinetic, will always oppose the direction of the force causing the sliding. Also, both coefficients of friction are always less than one, and the coefficient of static friction is usually greater than the coefficient of kinetic friction.

This means that it takes a greater force to get an object to start sliding across a surface than it does to keep the object sliding once it has already started. The figure following shows a graph of the force of friction versus the sliding force applied to an object.

Considering this graph in relation to our refrigerator example, if you start pushing on the refrigerator, the force of static friction will prevent sliding until you have applied enough force to overcome the stiction point. After this, the force of kinetic friction will give a constant opposition to the sliding, no matter how hard or fast you push.

Force of Friction (F_f) with Increasing Applied Force (F)

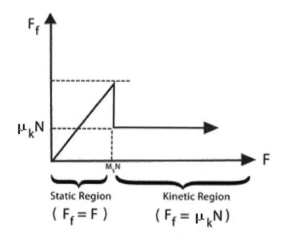

Energy
An object raised to a height above the ground will have an amount of stored energy known as **gravitational potential energy**. The higher an object is moved, the more potential it has. Gravitational potential energy is defined as: $PE = m * g * h$.

Here, m is the mass of the object, g is the acceleration of gravity (9.81 m/s^2), and h is the height of the object from the surface of the earth.

Sometimes, gravitational potential energy is represented by the letter U instead of PE.

Gravitational potential energy, like all types of energy, is given in units of joules (J) or foot-pounds-force (ft-lbf). You may notice that gravitational potential energy is simply the force of gravity on an object multiplied by the objects height.

Since the force of gravity, or weight, is given in units of Newtons, one joule is the same as one Newton multiplied by one meter (1J = 1Nm). When an object is dropped, its gravitational potential energy is converted into **kinetic energy**, which is defined as: $KE = \frac{1}{2} m * v^2$.

Here, m is again the mass of the object and v is the object's velocity.

Kinetic energy also has units of joules and is sometimes represented by the letter E instead of KE. Energy is always conserved, meaning it cannot be created or destroyed. This is known as the law of **conservation of energy**. The law of conservation of gravitational energy can be written as:
$PE + KE = m * g * h + \frac{1}{2} m * v^2 = $ constant.

However, all types of energy are always conserved, whether mechanical, electrical, chemical, nuclear, solar, etc. Even the power plants that supply our homes with electricity do not create energy; they simply convert kinetic, chemical, nuclear, or solar energy into electrical energy.

If an object is brought to a certain height, it has a particular amount of gravitational potential energy. When the object is dropped, its potential energy is converted to kinetic energy, so the amount of gravitational potential energy that the object had at its highest point will be exactly how much kinetic energy it has as it hits the ground (ignoring aero drag).

The law of conservation of energy applies to all objects in a gravitational field, so the velocity of a falling object will depend only on the height through which it has fallen and not the path. This means that the same laws used to find the speed of a falling baseball can also be used to find the speed of a rollercoaster.

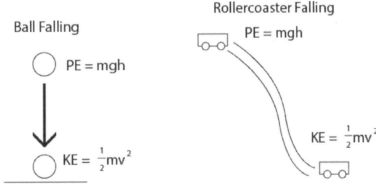

119

Work

In physics, the term **work** refers to a force applied over some distance: $W = F * d$.

F is the force being applied, and d is the distance of movement in the direction of the force.

It is important to remember that the distance measured is the **displacement** in the direction of the force, which is not the same as total distance traveled; displacement is the distance between the starting and ending points.

If you are holding a book and either keep it stationary or move it to the side, no work has been accomplished because you are pushing upward on the book and there has been no upward movement.

If you move the book upward, work has been done against gravity, and if you allow the book to move downward while holding it, you have done negative work because the movement was opposite the direction of the force you are applying.

In the case of downward movement, one can also say that gravity has done the work; the gravitational force is pulling the book downward in the same direction as the book's movement, so gravity has done positive work on the book.

Work is given in units of joules (J) or foot-pounds-force (ft-lbf). This is the same unit as energy because work can also be thought of as a change in the state of energy of an object, known as the **work-energy theorem**.

In our example of the book, if it weighs 1N and you lift it 1m upward, you have done 1 J of work, or added 1 J of gravitational potential energy. You can verify this by comparing the equations for work and potential energy. Since the force you are exerting to hold up the book is equal to the weight of the book, the work equation is the same as the equation for gravitational potential energy ($m * g * h$).

Power

Power is the rate at which work is done: $P = W/t$.

W is the amount of work done in joules (J) and t is the time over which the work was accomplished in seconds (s). One joule per second (J/s) is equal to a watt (W), the common metric unit of power.

Power can also be given in units of foot-pounds-force per second (ft-lbf/s) or horsepower (hp). One horsepower is equal to 550 ft-lb/s or 746 W. Work is force times distance, so if a force is being applied to an object to move it at a constant velocity, we can also say that power is force times velocity:
$P = F * d/t = F * v$.

F is force, and v is velocity either in meters per second (m/s) or feet per second (ft/s).

Simple Machines

These physics definitions of work and power can be counterintuitive. If you hold dumbbells in front of you with your arms outstretched, you will eventually grow tired. However, if the weights are not moving, according to the laws of physics, no work has been done and, no matter how long you hold the weights, no power will ever be used. Your physical exhaustion results not from the work done, but the force you have to apply to hold the weights in place.

This is the basis for the simple machines that we use to make our lives easier every day. **Simple machines** are devices that change the direction or magnitude of a force. The **mechanical advantage** of simple machine is defined as the output force divided by the force that is applied: $MA = F_{out}/F_{in}$.

F_{out} is the machine's output force or load and F_{in} is the force input or effort to the simple machine. The mechanical advantage is, in a sense, the percentage of the input force that is applied as the output of the simple machine. A simple machine does not do work or create power, instead work and power are said to be conserved, meaning that a simple machine can multiply force only by sacrificing displacement and speed.

Levers

The first type of simple machine we will look at is the lever. A **lever** is simply a beam with a pivot or hinge known as a **fulcrum**, which can either multiply the input force by sacrificing output travel distance or multiply distance and speed with a decreased output force. The mechanical advantage of lever is given by: $MA_{lever} = d_{in}/d_{out}$.

Here, d_{in} is the distance from the fulcrum to the point where the input force is applied, or input arm, and d_{out} is the output arm, or distance from the fulcrum to the point of the output force. Levers are divided into three types or classes: **first class**, **second class**, and **third class**.

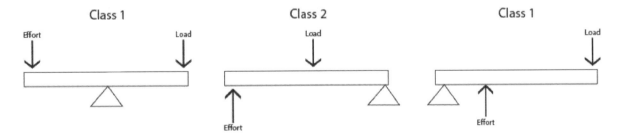

When an input force is applied to a lever, it creates a moment, or torque, about the fulcrum, which is then balanced by the output force. This means the input force multiplied by the input arm is equal to the output force multiplied by the output arm.

1. **First Class Lever**: The fulcrum is between the input and output forces, which are in opposite directions. A popular example of a first class lever is a seesaw. On a seesaw, when one person is in the air, their weight is applying a downward force on one end of the lever and the other person must apply an upward force to bring

them back to the earth. A seesaw has input and output arms of equal length, so the mechanical advantage is one, meaning the input and output force and the distances traveled by the two riders are equal.

A first class lever like this is said to have no mechanical advantage, or a mechanical advantage of one, because it merely changes the direction of the input force. If it is desired to multiply the input force, the input arm should be lengthened. This will give the lever a mechanical advantage greater than one.

Conversely, by lengthening the input arm, the output force will not move as far. If the output arm is longer, it will move faster and farther than the input arm, but a greater input force is required. A lever like this would have a mechanical advantage less than one.

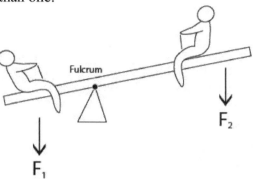

2. **Second Class Lever**: The input and output forces are on the same side of the fulcrum, with the output force closer to the fulcrum, meaning that a second class lever will always have a mechanical advantage greater than one. The most popular example of a second class lever is a wheelbarrow. The front wheel of a wheelbarrow acts as its fulcrum and the user lifts far behind the location of the load in order to lift very heavy objects.

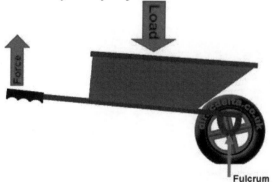

3. **Third Class Lever**: The input and output forces are on the same side of the fulcrum on a **third class lever** as well. In contrast to a second class lever, the input force of a third class lever is applied closer to the fulcrum than the load.

This means third class levers have a mechanical advantage less than one and are used to increase the output distance or speed. For example, take a swinging baseball bat: The batter places both hands near the end of the handle and swings;

the top hand moves faster than the other, so the slower hand acts as a fulcrum. The end which makes contact with the ball is moving very quickly when the ball is hit.

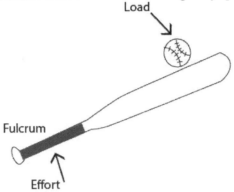

Inclined Planes

The **inclined plane** is another simple machine. Basic inclined planes are often used to do work against gravity, as is the case with a ramp. When an inclined plane is used to move an object upward, the user does not have to use as much force as if they lifted the object vertically upward.

However, the user must apply the force over a greater distance, so the work required is the same for both cases if we ignore friction. The mechanical advantage of an inclined plane is: $MA_{inclined\ plane} = L/H$.

L is the length of the inclined plane and H is the height, as shown in the figure below. This equation can be confusing when compared to our original mechanical advantage equation ($MA = F_{out}/F_{in}$), but in the case of an inclined plane, we can think of the output force as the force required if the load were lifted vertically upward, and the input force as the actual effort required when using the inclined plane.

It would seem that the most efficient inclined plane would have an extremely long length because this increases the mechanical advantage. However, increasing the length not only increases the travel distance up the ramp but also the strength requirement of the plane. This is similar to breaking a stick by bending it. If you have a very long twig, it can be easily broken in half.

Once the stick has been broken in half, the shorter resulting halves will be harder to break. If the process is repeated a few times, you may no longer be able to break the stick by hand. When an inclined plane is used to lift a load, the item being lifted applies a downward force to the ramp, bending and possibly breaking it if the ramp is too long or weak.

 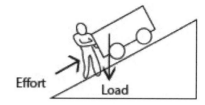

Inclined Plane

Screws

A **screw** is a specific application of the inclined plane; it is simply an inclined plane wrapped around a cylinder. If you look closely at a single-threaded screw, a triangle can be formed out of the threading by connecting consecutive teeth. The mechanical advantage of the screw will depend on the length of the tool used to turn the screw.

A screw can also be used for lifting heavy objects with the setup shown below, known as a **screw jack**. The mechanical advantage for this assembly is: $MA_{\text{screw jack}} = 2\pi R/P$.

Here, R is the torque arm, or distance from the center of the bolt (the fulcrum) and P is the distance between two consecutive teeth on the screw threading, known as the thread's pitch.

This mechanical advantage is found by considering the total distance that the input force must travel ($2\pi R$) and the total height that the screw will rise (P) in one turn of the input torque arm. Sometimes the mechanical advantage of only the screw is given, without specifying a tool or setup used to turn the screw.

In these cases, the radius of the shaft around which the inclined plane is wrapped is used as the torque arm r in the mechanical advantage equation.

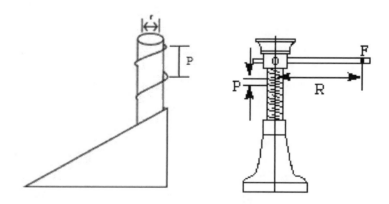

Wedges

The **wedge** is another variation of the inclined plane. A wedge can be thought of as two inclined planes placed back-to-back. Wedges are normally used for cutting and splitting as well as securing an object in place. An axe or knife is an example of a wedge used for cutting or splitting. A wedge is also used to secure the head of a hammer to its handle and to hold open doors as a doorstop. The mechanical advantage equation of a wedge differs only slightly from that for an inclined plane: $MA_{wedge} = L/t$.

The thickness, $t,$ is measured across the end of the wedge. Again, it would seem that a wedge should be as long and sharp as possible, but a thinner, sharper wedge not only is transversely weaker (to side-loading), but also has a tendency of binding when used to chop. For instance, if a log-splitting axe is too sharp, it can become lodged in the wood with the log flexing back onto the blade, increased friction and making the axe difficult to remove.

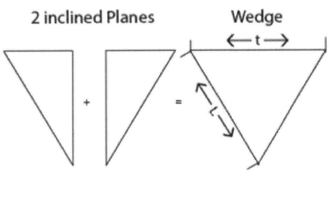

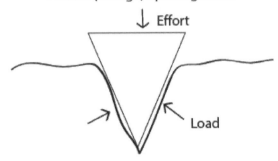

Pulleys and the Block and Tackle

The next type of simple machine we'll look at is the **pulley**. Pulleys are not used alone; they are used to support a cable, rope, belt, or chain, so we should discuss these items, which we will refer to simply as "cords" from now on, before trying to understand pulleys. Cords can be thought of simply as force transmitters.

However, unlike solid bodies and fluids, cords can only transmit pulling force, known as **tension**. If you try to bend or push on a cord it flexes, providing no resistance; if you secure a cord to an object and pull on it, though, it will transmit this pull as tension to the object to which it is attached.

When loaded, the tension throughout a cord is uniform, meaning that every piece of a cord along its length sees the exact same load. This is where the phrase, "A chain is only as strong as its weakest link" comes from. Each link in the chain will see the same load and be under the same amount of stress, so the entire chain can only hold the amount that the weakest link can hold before breaking.

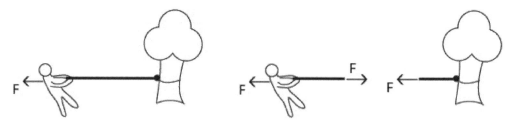

When you pull on a rope, the force is uniformly distributed through
the length of the rope as tension.

A **pulley** is a wheel and axle that supports a cord and, in doing so, changes the direction of cord's orientation and therefore the direction of the tension in the cord. Although pulleys have some frictional losses, they are small enough that we can ignore them and say that the tension in the cord is uniform. This means that the pulling force's direction is changed while its magnitude stays the same. This means that a single pulley offers no mechanical advantage ($F_{in} = F_{out}$ so $MA_{pulley} = 1$).

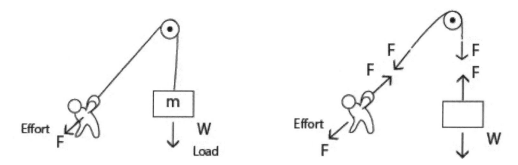

When a pulley is used to suspend an object, the tension in the rope is
uniform and equal to the weight of the object.

However, a series of pulleys, known as a block and tackle, can be used to give a mechanical advantage and make it possible to more easily lift heavy objects. When the input force is applied to a single cord, the mechanical advantage of a block and tackle can be found by counting the number of cord segments whose tension is being applied to lift the object: $MA_{b\&t} = N$.

Here, N is the number of cord segments extending from the moving output block, as shown in the pictures below. Again, this mechanical advantage comes at the cost of moving distance, so if the mechanical advantage is 4, then the output block will only move one quarter of the distance traveled by the input force.

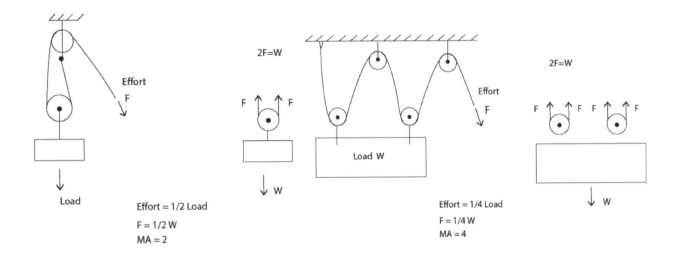

Effort
F

Load

Effort = 1/2 Load

F = 1/2 W

MA = 2

2F=W

F ↑ ↑ F

↓ W

2F=W

Effort
F

Load W

Effort = 1/4 Load

F = 1/4 W

MA = 4

F ↑ ↑ F   F ↑ ↑ F

↓ W

The Wheel and Axle

We said that a pulley is a wheel and axle, but the wheel and axle is, in its own right, a simple machine. **Wheel and axle** refers to two cylinders that are attached to each other coaxially that are allowed to rotate about their center, as shown below. The wheel and axle can be thought of as a variation of the lever, with the fulcrum at the center and the forces applied tangentially to the surface of the wheel and the axle, sometimes using belts or rope wrapped around the wheel and/or axle. In this way, the wheel and axle creates a continuous lever. The mechanical advantage of a wheel and axle assembly is given by:

$MA_{w\&a} = R_{wheel}/R_{axle}$

Here, R_{wheel} and R_{axle} are the radii of the wheel and axle, respectively.

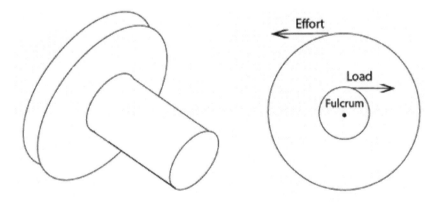

However, an axle does not have to have only one wheel and each wheel does not have to be the same size. The wheels on a car are the same size, but sometimes wheel and axles are required to turn various machine parts at different speeds. For this, assemblies like the one shown below are necessary. The mechanical advantage between two different wheels can be found as: $MA_{wheels} = R_{in}/R_{out}$.

Here, R_{in} and R_{out} are the radii of the input wheel and output wheel, respectively. The mechanical advantage of the wheel and axle and two-wheel assembly are both found by comparing the input and output moments about the axis; the input and output torques must be equal. Remember again that this mechanical advantage will be gained by sacrificing the distance traveled.

For instance, if the input wheel has a radius four times as large as the output, the mechanical advantage will be four. This means the output force will be four times as large as the input, but the circumference of the output wheel is a quarter of that of the input wheel, so a belt attached to the output wheel will turn only a quarter as far as one attached to the input wheel.

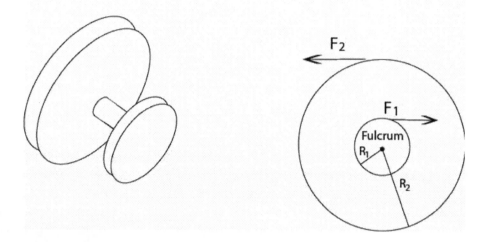

Gears

The rotation and torque of a wheel can be transmitted a great distance by connecting two wheels with a belt or chain, as shown below The mechanical advantage of this setup is given by: $MA_{gears} = R_{out} / R_{in}$.

R_{out} and R_{in} are again the output and input radii, respectively. Notice that this mechanical advantage is the inverse of the mechanical advantage between two wheels on the same axle (MA_{wheels}) and is denoted as MA_{gears}. The reason that a belt or chain assembly's mechanical advantage is represented by MA_{gears} is that this type of pulley assembly is the same basic concept as two gears; it is two disks rotating with the same tangential velocity at their contact point.

However, two gears will rotate in opposite directionsThe only major difference between two meshed gears and two pulleys connected by a belt or chain is that two consecutive gears will rotate in opposite directions while the pulleys connected by a belt or chain will rotate in the same diection. **Gears** are simply interlocking wheels with their **effective radii** given by the point at which the two wheels have the same velocity.

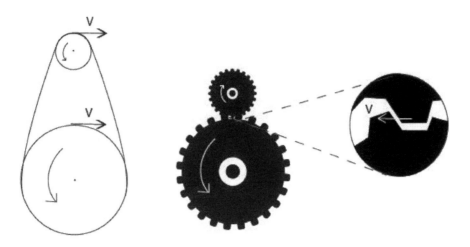

Effective radii at two gears are given by the point at which their linear velocities are equal. Pulleys connected by a belt or chain are two discs that turn with the same velocity at their radii, just like gears, and the assembly's mechanical advantage is calculated the same way as a pair of gears. However, a pair of gears will rotate in opposite directions.

To find the mechanical advantage of a long **gear train**, or series of gears interlocked together, we only need to worry about the input and output gear radii, not the radii of the gears in between, as long as they are interlocked and not on the same shaft.

Again, if the output gear has a radius four times that of the input gear, the mechanical advantage will be four but the output gear will only rotate once for every four rotations of the input gear.

For two interlocking gears, the force applied at the effective radius, or meshing point, is the same for both gears, similar to the tension being constant throughout a rope or belt in the pulley assemblies. Since the gears are different radii, this creates different moments on the two gears. If the input gear is driving a larger output gear, the output force is greater than the input and the assembly is called a torque-multiplier or speed-reduction assembly. If the output gear is smaller than the input, the assembly is a speed-multiplying or torque-reducing assembly.

$$MA = \frac{Ru}{R3} \; x \frac{R3}{R2} \; x \frac{R2}{R1} = \frac{R4}{R1} = \frac{R \, out}{R \, in}$$

Fluids and Hydraulics

If a force needs to be transmitted a great distance, it may not be convenient to use any of the mechanical simple machines discussed above. Instead, fluids can be used to transmit the force through hydraulic and pneumatic systems. The term fluid is not synonymous with liquid. A **fluid** is any material that conforms to the shape of its container and is not compressible, so we consider any liquid or gas to be an incompressible fluid.

In fluids, we define **pressure** as a force per unit area, given in pounds per square inch (psi); Pascals (Pa), which is the equivalent of one Newton (N) per square meter (m^2); or **inches of mercury** (in Hg), which is defined as the pressure exerted by a one-inch high column of liquid mercury.

The principle of transmission of pressure, also known as **Pascal's law**, states that pressure applied to one part of the fluid will be distributed evenly to the entire rest of the fluid. In large containers of liquid, the pressure relies on the pressure applied at the surface as well as the depth within the container, so the pressure increases deeper in the container due to the weight of the water.

However, in containers of gas or shallow containers of liquids, the effects of gravity can be ignored and the pressure is constant throughout the container. This principle is utilized in **hydraulics** through the setup shown in the picture below.

In this simplified hydraulic system, one piston is applying a pressure that is equal to the input force spread over the area of the piston's face. This pressure is distributed throughout the fluid, so the face of the second piston will see the same force per unit area. This relationship is stated mathematically as:

$$P_{in} = P_{out}$$
$$F_{in} / A_{in} = F_{out} / A_{out}$$

P_{in} is the pressure on the face of the input piston, which is the input force divided by the area of the input piston's face and is equal to the output pressure P_{out}. Since the output piston in this case is larger, the output force will be greater. For this dual-piston setup, we can define a mechanical advantage by dividing the output force by the input (the definition of mechanical advantage): $MA_{pistons} = A_{out} / A_{in}$.

Remember, this mechanical advantage is gained through decreasing the output motion, so if the output piston has an area four times that of the input, the mechanical advantage will be four, so the output force will be four times the input; however, the output piston will only move a quarter of the distance of the input piston's travel, assuming incompressibility of the fluid.

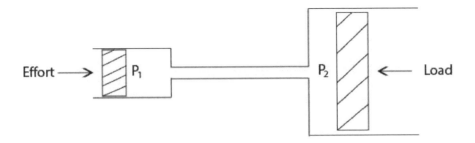

Basic Piston setup of Hydraulic System
The input force is distributed over the face of the input piston and transferred
to the fluid as pressure, which is applies an output force to the second piston.

This difference in piston motion can also be explained by considering volume displacement of the fluid. When the input piston moves, it displaces a volume of fluid equal to the area of the piston multiplied by the distance of the piston's motion.

This volume displaced causes the output piston to move to make room for the volume entering the cylinder, but since the output piston has a larger area, it will not need to move as far to displace the same amount of fluid.

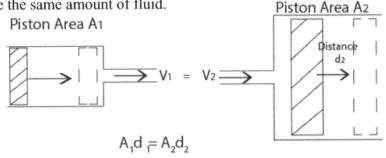

$$A_1 d_1 = A_2 d_2$$

The movement of the pistons in the hydraulic system can also be explained
by fluid displacement. The volume of fluid displaced by the movement of
the first piston ($V_1 = A_1 d_1$) flows into the second cylinder ($V_1 = V_2$) and
causes the piston to move to make room for the incoming fluid.

This volume displacement concept can also be applied to a fluid flowing through a pipe. When a fluid is flowing through a pipe, mass must be conserved, meaning that no amount of fluid is gathering anywhere in the pipe; the amount of fluid flowing into the pipe is equal to the amount flowing out.

Since the flow is constant through all points in the pipe, the flow velocity must increase whenever the cross-sectional area of the pipe decreases. Mathematically, the law of **conservation of mass** is stated as:

$$Q_1 = Q_2$$
$$v_1 * A_1 = v_2 * A_2$$

Here, Q_1 and Q_2 are the volumetric flow rates of the fluid, v_1 and v_2 are the velocities of fluid particles, and A_1 and A_2 are the cross-sectional areas of the pipe at points 1 and 2, respectively.

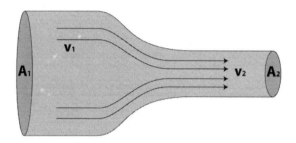

Energy must also be conserved in the flow of a fluid, just like any other body subjected to gravity. Unlike solid bodies, however, fluids also have a defined pressure energy. This means that between any two points, the sum of a fluid's pressure, kinetic, and potential energies must remain constant. Mathematically, this is stated in a force per unit area basis:

$$p + \tfrac{1}{2}\rho v^2 + \rho g h = \text{constant}$$
$$p_1/\rho + v_1^2/2 + g\,h_1 = p_2/\rho + v_2^2/2 + g\,h_2$$

Here, p is pressure, ρ is the density of the fluid (which we assume remains constant), v is the velocity of the fluid, g is the acceleration of gravity (9.81 m/s^2 or 32.2 ft/s^2), and h is the height of the fluid.

This relationship is known as **Bernoulli's principle** and can be applied to any points along a streamline. A **streamline** is an imaginary line through a smoothly flowing fluid that is always tangential to the fluid's velocity, and can be thought of as a line that would follow the path of a particle flowing through the fluid.

Mechanical Comprehension Practice Test

1. A person moves forward ten steps and then backwards ten steps. What is the total distance traveled?
   a) -10 steps.
   b) 0 steps.
   c) 10 steps.
   d) 20 steps.

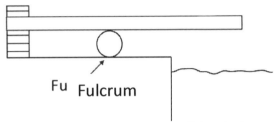

2. A springboard is a diving board made out of a flexible platform that acts like a spring and is held stationary by a hinge on one end with an adjustable fulcrum, so that a person can dive off the other end, as shown in the picture above. What will happen if the fulcrum is moved away from the diver?
   a) The board will be stiffer.
   b) The board will flex more under the weight of the diver.
   c) Fulcrum position makes no difference.
   d) The platform will be less likely to break.

3. A car travels 60 miles south in one hour, and then 90 miles north in two hours. What is the total displacement during this time?
   a) -30 miles.
   b) 0 miles.
   c) 30 miles.
   d) 150 miles.

4. For the car described in problem #3, what is the average speed during the first hour of travel?
   a) -60 mph.
   b) 1 mph.
   c) 50 mph.
   d) 60 mph.

5. For the car described in problem #3, what is the average speed during the 3 hours of travel?
   a) -10 mph.
   b) 0 mph.
   c) 10 mph.
   d) 50 mph.

6. For the car in problem #3, what is the average velocity during the 3 hours of travel, if we define north as the positive direction?
   a) -10 mph.
   b) -1 mph.
   c) 1 mph.
   d) 10 mph.

7. A 10 kg person stands on a scale. Approximately what will the scale read?
   a) 10 N.
   b) 32 N.
   c) 98 N.
   d) 196 N.

8. A 10 kg person travels to the Moon, which has a smaller acceleration due to gravity than the Earth. What will happen to the person's mass?
   a) The person's mass will decrease.
   b) The person's mass will stay the same.
   c) The person's mass will increase.
   d) It is impossible to tell from this information.

9. A 10 kg person travels to the Moon, which has a smaller acceleration due to gravity than the Earth. What will happen to the person's weight?
   a) The person's weight will decrease.
   b) The person's weight will stay the same.
   c) The person's weight will increase.
   d) It is impossible to tell from this information.

10. A person travels to a distant planet and finds that their weight has increased relative to their weight on Earth. Assuming the person's mass has not changed, what can we say about the planet's radius?
   a) The planet's radius is smaller than that of Earth.
   b) The planet's radius is equal to that of the Earth.
   c) The planet's radius is larger than that of the Earth.
   d) It is impossible to tell from this information.

11. What force is required to accelerate a 10 kg object from rest to 10 m/s in 5 seconds? (Assume no resistive forces.)
   a) 15 N.
   b) 20 N.
   c) 100 N.
   d) 500 N.

12. A 50 kg object begins at rest on a surface with a static coefficient of friction at 0.6 and a kinetic coefficient of friction at 0.5. If you push horizontally on the object with a force of 27 N, how quickly will it move across the surface? (Assume that the object does not tip over.)
   a) 0 m/s.
   b) 5 m/s.
   c) 20 m/s.
   d) 30 m/s.

13. Which of these best describes the gear train above?
   a) Torque-multiplier.
   b) Speed-multiplier.
   c) Frequency-multiplier.
   d) None of the above.

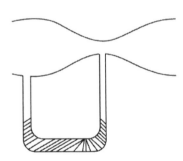

14. The figure above shows an air duct that narrows at a point. A U-tube is attached as shown and the bottom is filled with water. What will happen to the water when air starts flowing through the duct?
   a) The left side will go up and the right side will go down.
   b) Both sides will go down.
   c) The left side will go down and the right side will go up.
   d) Both sides will go up.

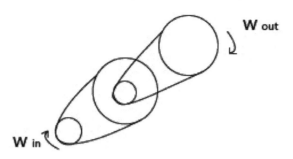

15. Which of these describes the pulley train shown above?
   a) Rotation-inverter.
   b) Speed-multiplier.
   c) Torque-multiplier.
   d) None of the above.

16. To have the best leverage in the scissors above, you should:
   a) Hold the scissors at D and cut at A.
   b) Hold the scissors at D and cut at B.
   c) Hold the scissors at C and cut at A.
   d) Hold the scissors at C and cut at B.

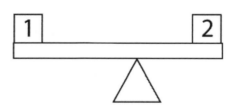

17. Which of the objects in the picture above weighs more?
   a) Object 1.
   b) Object 2.
   c) They weigh the same amount.
   d) It is impossible to tell.

18. Which of these statements is true about a car's transmission?
    a) Higher gears have a higher mechanical advantage.
    b) Lower gears have a higher mechanical advantage.
    c) All the gears have the same mechanical advantage.
    d) The mechanical advantage depends on the weight of the car.

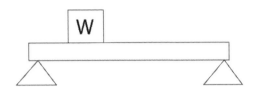

19. In the picture above, does the support on the left or right carry more of the object's weight?
    a) Left supports more weight.
    b) Right supports more weight.
    c) They carry the same amount of weight.
    d) It is impossible to tell.

20. Three cubes of equal volume are put in a hot oven. The cubes are made of three materials: wood, iron, and silver. Which cube will heat the fastest?
    a) The wooden cube.
    b) The iron cube.
    c) The silver cube.
    d) The cubes all heat up at the same rate.

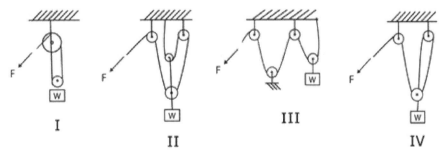

21. Which of block and tackle pictured above requires the least effort to lift a weight of W?
    a) I.
    b) II.
    c) III.
    d) IV.

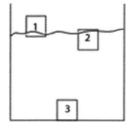

22. What can be said about the three objects shown above in a tank of water?
   a) Object 3 weighs the most.
   b) Object 1 has the lowest density.
   c) Objects 1 and 2 have the same density.
   d) None of the above.

23. Two gears create a mechanical advantage of 4:1 and the larger gear has 24 teeth. How many teeth does the pinion have?
   a) 6 teeth.
   b) 12 teeth.
   c) 24 teeth.
   d) 96 teeth.

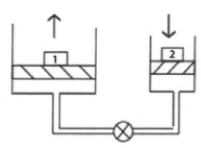

24. In the hydraulic system shown above, the valve is originally closed and the two objects are level. When the valve is opened, the object on the right begins to move downward and the object on the left moves upward. What can be said about the two objects?
   a) Object 1 weighs more.
   b) Object 2 weighs more.
   c) The objects weigh the same amount.
   d) It is impossible to tell from this information.

25. The figure above is a simplified model of the camshaft in a car's engine. The pulley attached to the crankshaft is of half the diameter of the pulley attached to the camshaft. About how far must the crankshaft turn before the camshaft pushes the valve all the way open?

    a) 90 degrees.
    b) 180 degrees.
    c) 270 degrees.
    d) 540 degrees.

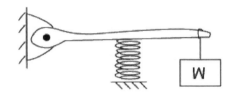

26. The picture above shows a hinged arm attached to a weight and being held horizontal by a spring. If the weight is moved to the left (closer to the hinge), what will happen?

    a) The spring will compress more.
    b) The spring will extend.
    c) Nothing.
    d) It is impossible to tell.

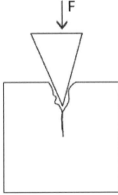

27. The picture above shows an axe splitting a piece of wood. What type of simple machine is this?

    a) Lever.
    b) Blade.
    c) Inclined plane.
    d) None of these.

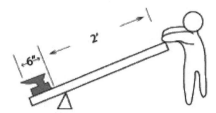

28. The picture above shows a person lifting a heavy object with a lever. What is the mechanical advantage?

    a) 0.25.

    b) 0.3.

    c) 3.

    d) 4.

29. Which of these best describes the gear train shown above?

    a) Torque-multiplier.

    b) Speed-multiplier.

    c) Frequency-multiplier.

    d) None of the above.

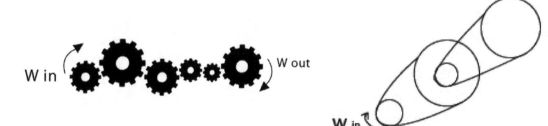

30. If the input gear on the left has the same diameter as the input pulley on the right and the output gear on the left has the same diameter as the output pulley on the right, which assembly gives the higher mechanical advantage?

    a) The gear train on the left.

    b) The pulley train on the right.

    c) The assemblies have the same mechanical advantage.

    d) It is impossible to tell.

Mechanical Comprehension Practice Test – Answers

1. **d) 20 steps**. Total distance traveled does not take direction into account, so we can add the two distances: $10 + 10 = 20$ steps.

2. **b) The board will flex more under the weight of the diver**. The distance between the fulcrum and the diver is being lengthened, so the torque arm is being increased; the weight of the diver will apply a greater moment to the platform, resulting in the platform flexing a greater amount.

    You can also consider the two extremes of the fulcrum either being adjusted directly underneath the diver or as far away from the diver as possible. If the fulcrum is underneath the diver the board will not flex at all, and if the fulcrum is the farthest point away from the diver the board will flex the maximum amount.

    This means that the board flexes more as the fulcrum is adjusted away from the diver. Since the board is flexing more, it would be more likely to break because there is a greater moment.

3. **c) 30 miles**. Displacement is the distance between the starting and ending points, so we cannot simply add the two distances together. If we take north as the positive direction, the car moves 60 miles in the positive direction and then 90 miles in the negative direction.

    Adding these values, $60 + (-90) = 60 - 90 = -30$ miles. However, displacement is always positive. Displacement is not a vector, but a scalar. It is just the distance between the start and end points, NOT the vector distance between the two points.

4. **d) 60 mph**. Speed is distance traveled divided by time and does not take direction into account. In this case, the car travels 60 miles in one hour, 60 miles / 1 hour = 60 miles per hour.

5. **d) 50 mph**. Speed is a scalar value, so it does not take direction into account. Average speed is distance traveled divided by time (x/t), so we first find the distance traveled, $60 + 90 = 150$ miles, then the total time, $1 + 2 = 3$ hours, and finally divide the distance by time, $150/3 = 50$ miles per hour.

    While it is also possible to find the average speed during the two legs of the trip and calculate a weighted average, this is much more complicated and reduces to the same equation.

6. **d) 10 mph**. Notice in this question we have to define a positive direction because the question asks for a vector value, which has a magnitude and direction. Similar to problem #4, we must first find the total displacement of the car, which is 30 miles. Remember that this is north, which has been defined as the positive direction.

Like average speed, average velocity is distance divided by time, 30 miles/3 hours = 10 mph, and since the distance traveled is in the positive direction, the average velocity will also be positive: +30/3 = +10mph.-30

Again, we could also find the average velocity during each leg of the trip and find a weighted average, but this is even more complicated when working with vector values and still reduces to the same equation of total distance divided by total time.

7. **c) 98 N.** A scale measures weight, and since it is the earth's gravitational pull on the object which is being weighed, the force of gravity is the mass of the object times the constant acceleration due to gravity (9.8 m/s^2). W = mg = 10 * 9.8 = 98 N

8. **b) The person's mass will stay the same.** Mass is a scalar vector depends on the density and volume of an object, both of which will stay constant. A person's mass will stay the same no matter what planet they are on.

9. **a) The person's weight will decrease.** Weight is a measurement of force, so it is a vector value which has a magnitude that depends on mass and acceleration. We already found in problem #8 that the person's mass will not change, so their weight will be proportional to the acceleration of gravity.

    Since the acceleration due to gravity on the moon is less than that of the earth, the acceleration of gravity will decrease when the person travels to the moon, meaning their weight will also decrease.

10. **d) It is impossible to tell from this information.** Since the person's weight has increased, the acceleration of gravity on this distant planet is higher than that on Earth. It is tempting to say this must be a smaller planet. However, we cannot say anything about the planet's radius because gravitational force depends on both the mass and distance from the center of an object.

    Acceleration due to gravity on a planet depends on the planet's mass and radius; it varies directly with mass and proportionally to the inverse square of the radius (m/r^2). If this planet has the same mass as the Earth, its radius must be smaller so that the planet is denser than the earth. If the radius of the planet is the same as the Earth's, it must have a larger mass and density. However, we are not given any of this information, so the only thing we can say is that the value of m/r^2 for the planet is larger than the Earth's.

11. **b) 20 N.** This problem involves Newton's second law ($F = ma$). To find the force required, we must first calculate the desired acceleration, which is the rate of change of velocity,
    $a = \Delta v/\Delta t = 10/5 = 2$ m/s^2. Newton's second law states that $F = ma = 10 * 2 = 20$ N.

12. **a) 0 m/s.** The key to this question is that the object "begins at rest". In order for an object at rest to begin moving, the maximum static friction force must first be overcome,
    $F_{f,s} = \mu_s * N = 0.6 * 50 = 30$ N.

Since the force being applied is less than the "stiction" force, the object will not move. The force of friction in this case is equal to the 27 N being applied. Had the force been greater than 30 N, the object would move, a kinetic friction force of $F_{f,k} = \mu_k * N = 0.5 * 50 = 25$ N would resist the motion, and the speed at steady state would be much more difficult to find.

13. **b) Speed-multiplier**. Remember that in a gear train it is only necessary to look at the input and output gears. Since the input gear is larger than the output, the output gear will turn faster, making this a speed-multiplying gear train.

14. **c) The left side will go down and the right side will go up**. Air flowing through the duct will have to speed up at the narrow portion. According to Bernoulli's principle, the pressure in the air will decrease when the speed increases, so the pressure on the right side of the U-tube will be less than the pressure on the left side. This will push the water downward in the left side of the pipe and, since the volume of the water will stay constant (the water is incompressible), the water in the right side will rise.

15. **b) Torque-multiplier**. Pulley trains which include a wheel and axle like this one are not as simple as gear trains; you can't just look at the input and output pulleys. Instead, you have to look at each step of the pulleys. Fortunately, both steps of this system decrease the speed and increase torque, so this assembly is a torque-multiplier.

16. **b) Hold the scissors at D and cut at B**. For the best leverage, the input arm should be long and the output arm should be short. This means the load should be close to the fulcrum at B and the effort should be far from the fulcrum at D.

17. **b) Object 2**. Object 1 is farther away from the fulcrum, giving it a greater torque arm and therefore higher mechanical advantage that object 2. Since the lever is horizontal, the moments cause by the two objects must be equal, $F_1R_1 = F_2R_2$. $R_1 > R_2$, so therefore $F_2 > F_1$.

18. **b) Lower gears have a higher mechanical advantage**. When driving a car, the transmission is shifted into higher gears when the car is moving faster, so the higher gears are able to produce a higher speed at the expense of torque, meaning they have less of a mechanical advantage. If a person puts a manual transmission in a high gear and tries to move a car from rest, the engine speed will drop and the engine will most likely not have enough power to start because there is not enough of a mechanical advantage. This can also break the car's clutch.

19. **a) Left supports more weight**. The support on the left will carry more of the object's weight. Several approaches can be taken to analyze this problem.

If the support on the left is treated as a fulcrum and the support on the right as a force, similar to a class 2 lever, the force will not have to be large because it has a high mechanical advantage.

However, if the support on the right is treated as a fulcrum and the support on the left treated as an effort force, the force will not have much of a mechanical advantage.

The question is analogous to finding which object weighs more on a balance, as shown below. The weight on the left represents the reaction force of the support on the left in the original question and the weight on the right represents the reaction force of the support on the right.

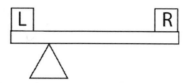

You can also think of the two extremes; if the weight is all the way to the left over the left support, the right support can be removed because it carries no load. Similarly, if the object is all the way on the right side, the right support carries the entire load. Since the object is closer to the left, the left support should carry more of the weight.

20. **c) The silver cube**. The speed at which the cubes will heat up depends on their thermal conductivity. Wood does not have a very high thermal conductivity. In metals, thermal conductivity generally follows the same trend as electrical conductivity; metals with high electrical conductivity have high thermal conductivity. This means the silver cube has the highest coefficient of thermal conductivity and will therefore heat the fastest.

21. **B) II**. Looking closely at the figure: the two pulleys above the weight in II are attached, and the weight in setup II has four rope segments extending from it, so the mechanical advantage is four and $F = W/4$. Setups I and III have two rope segments extending from the weight, giving a mechanical advantage of 2, and setup IV has three rope segments extending from it, so setup IV's mechanical advantage is 3.

22. **b) Object 1 has the lowest density**. How high an object floats in water depends on that object's density. The objects are acted on by the force of gravity, which depends on the objects mass and a buoyancy force that depends on the volume of the liquid displaced. If the question stated that the three objects had the same volume, then object 3 would be the heaviest because it has the highest density and density is mass per unit volume. However, the problem does not state this and the height at which an object floats only gives its density.

23. **a) 6 teeth**. The pinion refers to the smaller of the two gears, so whether the mechanical advantage is 1:4 or 4:1, the pinion will have one quarter the number of teeth as the gear.

24. d) It is impossible to tell from this information. Though it is tempting to say object 2 weighs more, this hydraulic system gives the force applied to the piston on the right a mechanical advantage, so object 2 could actually weigh the same or less than object 1 and still push object 1 upward. Remember, the weight of object 1 is spread over a greater area, causing less pressure, while the weight of object 2 is concentrated on a smaller area and causes greater pressure.

25. d) 540 degrees. It is important to note first that the lower pulley attached to the crankshaft is rotating clockwise. This means that the camshaft is also rotating clockwise. The camshaft must turn 270 degrees (3/4 turn) before the cam is aligned with the valve stem so it is pushed as far down as it will go. The crankshaft turns at twice the speed of the camshaft, so it must rotate twice as far, 540 degrees (1.5 turns).

26. b) The spring will extend. This is a class three lever, where the weight is the load and the spring is the effort. If the weight is moved to the left, the load's torque arm is shortened and the weight has less leverage. This means the spring does not have to apply as much force and therefore expands.

27. c) Inclined plane. The axe in the picture is a wedge. Remember that a wedge is a type of inclined plane.

28. d) 4. The mechanical advantage of the lever is the length of the input arm divided by the length of the output arm (d_{in}/d_{out}), but the two lengths must be in the same units first. The input arm is two feet or 24 inches and the output arm is 6 inches, which is half a foot. Either way, $24/6 = 2/.5 = 4$

29. . Normally, it is only necessary to consider the input and output gears. However, in this gear train three consecutive gears are touching, which means that this gear train will not be able to turn since two consecutive gears should turn in opposite directions.

30. b) The pulley train on the right. The pulley system has a greater mechanical advantage. For the gear train, the mechanical advantage can be found from the diameters of the input and output gears. The pulley system has two steps, both of which are torque-multipliers. The pulley system's input and output pulleys may have the same diameter of the gear train's input and output gears, but the wheel and axle in the pulley system give it a greater mechanical advantage.

Conclusion

At Accepted, Inc. we strive to help you reach your goals. We hope this guide gave you the information to not only score well but to exceed any previous expectations. Our goal is to keep it concise, show you a few test tricks along the way, and to ultimately help you succeed in your goals. Please let us know if we've truly prepared you for the exam and if don't mind including your test score we'd be thankful for that too! Please send us an email to feedback@acceptedinc.com.

Remember – Study Smarter. Score Higher. Get Accepted!

-Accepted, Inc.-

Made in the USA
Middletown, DE
01 August 2015